Cases in Finance

DAVID F. SCOTT, JR.
Professor of Finance
Texas Tech University

JOHN D. MARTIN
Associate Professor of Finance
Virginia Polytechnic Institute
and State University

J. WILLIAM PETTY
Associate Professor of Finance
Texas Tech University

ARTHUR J. KEOWN
Assistant Professor of Finance
Virginia Polytechnic Institute
and State University

PRENTICE-HALL, INC., Englewood Cliffs, N.J. 07632

Library of Congress Cataloging in Publication Data
Main entry under title:

Cases in finance.

1. Corporations - Finance - Case studies.
2. Business enterprises - Finance - Case studies.
I. Scott, David F. (date)
HG4026.C283   658.1'5   76-48748
ISBN   0-13-115337-4

ISBN 0-13-115337-4

Printed in the United States of America

10   9   8   7   6   5   4   3   2

Prentice-Hall International, Inc., London
Prentice-Hall of Australia Pty. Limited, *Sydney*
Prentice-Hall of Canada, Ltd., *Toronto*
Prentice-Hall of India Private Limited, *New Delhi*
Prentice-Hall of Japan, Inc., *Tokyo*
Prentice-Hall of Southeast Asia Pte. Ltd., *Singapore*
Whitehall Books Limited, Wellington, *New Zealand*

To our wives, Peggy, Sally, Donna, and Barbara,
and our families.
Their encouragements assured the
completion of this book.

Contents

Preface

The Case Method of Instruction

In order to truly understand problems of the financial manager and the role of financial theory in the real world, it is necessary for you as the student to actually experience real world problems. It is the purpose of the case method of study to expose you to actual decision making situations in the hope that this will provide you with greater insight into the problems of the financial manager in addition to improving your decision making ability. Since it is impossible for you to gain actual business experience in the classroom, the case method of instruction becomes a valuable tool in simulating the functioning of the financial manager.

In the past, you probably have been exposed to problems rather than cases. The difference between problems and cases is more than merely length. In cases, the business situation is described giving you a feel for the conditions, attitudes and practices of a particular company. Moreover, the financial situation being examined will be of a more complex nature than those you might have experienced in previous problem exercises. Additionally, cases differ from problems in three major respects. First, there is usually room for more than one correct answer. The correct answer depends upon the assumptions being made and in many cases there is room for varying assumptions. Secondly, whereas problems traditionally deal with only one aspect of a financial problem, cases recognize the complexity of the various financial problems and portray them in this state. It is for this reason that cases in finance generally require you to answer multiple and interacting questions in attempting to solve a problem.

Finally, in many cases you will find irrelevant information, just as in the real world, which requires you to differentiate between relevant and irrelevant facts in solving the problem.

With this in mind the case method approach should provide you with a broad learning experience as decision making experience is gained through the simulation of the financial business environment. Additionally, it should enable you to focus on the role of financial theory in actual business situations. In the end, it must be added that learning by the case method is an individual proposition, requiring a maximum effort, and so the value of the educational experience depends upon the effort put into it.

We wish to express sincere gratitude to those who have offered suggestions for the improvement of this text. Prof. Donald L. Stevens, University of Tennessee, Prof. David W. Cole, Ohio State University, and Prof. Dwight C. Anderson, Arizona State University, reviewed the manuscript at various stages and provided constructive ideas that were valuable to the authors.

D.F.S./J.D.M./J.W.P./A.J.K.

Cases
in
Finance

Section 1

Financial Analysis and Planning

Case 1

ABINGTON-HILL TOYS, INC.

(Part I: Financial Ratio Analysis)

On December 2, 1976, Vernon Albright assumed the position of president of the Abington-Hill Toy Company (AH), following the death of Lewis Hill, the last of the original founders of the firm. Neither Abington nor Hill had a son or daughter who was interested in taking over the firm's management. The financial condition of the firm had deteriorated during the final years of Hill's control; however, the firm's owners [1] felt that the company's prospects were good if a capable manager could be found to take over the leadership. A key concern of the owners was the lack of financial planning and general crisis-to-crisis pattern, which had characterized the firm's operation in recent years.

It was decided to seek a manager from outside the firm, who, in the owner's opinion, could reshape the company into the prosperous concern it once had been. Advertisements placed in a number of trade journals provided the owners with a list of six individuals who were willing and apparently capable of rebuilding AH. After extensive correspondence and several personal interviews with each of the applicants, Vernon Albright was chosen to head the firm.

---

[1] The firm is closely held, with 85 percent of the stock held by the combined Abington and Hill families. The remaining minority interest is primarily held by company employees who acquired it through the company stock option plan.

One of the first actions of the new president was to hire a company comptroller.[2] David Hartly, an assistant comptroller of a major electric appliance manufacturing firm, was hired and took over his duties on December 28, 1976. Hartly had been with that company since receiving his MBA in 1967 and had moved up in the comptroller's office to assistant to the comptroller in charge of general accounts and budgeting. His experience in budgetary procedures was viewed with particular favor by Albright in light of AH's recent financial problems.

Hartly's first task was to undertake a complete analysis of the firm's financial condition. Specifically, Albright had requested a statement of the firm's condition, including an enumeration of specific strengths and weaknesses. Also, he requested a brief statement of a feasible solution to the firm's most pressing problems.

QUESTIONS

1. Using ratio analysis and a statement of sources and uses of funds, prepare Hartly's statement of financial condition. (Financial statements are found in Exhibit 1 and industry standard ratios in Exhibit 2.)

2. Based on your analysis, what areas of the firm's operations are in greatest need of immediate attention? Prepare a planned course of action for the solution of the firm's most pressing problems.

---

[2]In the past, Hill had handled most of the comptroller functions with the assistance of the firm's chief accountant, Jerald Cohen, who had been with the firm for the 28 years of its existence and planned to retire within the year. He agreed to remain with the firm, at the request of the owners, until the new president could be selected and the company was on its feet. However, Cohen was in poor health and would probably be forced to retire within the year.

EXHIBIT 1

Abington-Hill Toys, Inc.

Comparative Balance Sheets
December 31, 1975 and 1976

	December 31, 1975	December 31, 1976
Cash	$ 50,000	$ 10,000
Accounts receivable	100,000	120,000
Inventory	150,000	150,000
Total current assets	$ 300,000	$ 280,000
Plant and equipment	$1,200,000	$1,480,000
Less: Allowance for depreciation	(500,000)	(560,000)
Total fixed assets	$ 700,000	$ 920,000
Total assets	$1,000,000	$1,200,000
Accounts payable	$ 40,000	$ 42,000
Short-term notes	50,000	224,000
Accrued expenses	20,000	24,000
Total current liabilities	110,000	290,000
Long-term debt	200,000	200,000
Common stock ($10 par)	200,000	200,000
Capital surplus	490,000	510,000
	$1,000,000	$1,200,000

Income Statement
For Year Ended December 31, 1976

	Actual 1976
Sales	$1,200,000[3]
Cost of goods sold	900,000
	$ 300,000
Operating expense:	
Variable cash operating expense	$ 84,000
Fixed cash operating expense	30,000
Depreciation	60,000
	$ 174,000
Net income before interest and taxes	126,000
Interest	39,600
Net income before taxes	$ 86,400
Taxes (50%)	43,200
Net income	$ 43,200

[3] 60% credit sales

EXHIBIT 2

Standard Industry Ratios

	Industry[4]
Current ratio	3.50X's
Acid-test ratio	1.50X's
Average collection period	60.0 days
Inventory turnover (COGS to ending inventory)	5.00X's
Fixed asset turnover	1.43X's
Total asset turnover	1.00X's
Debt ratio (total debt to total assets)	45.0%
Times interest earned (overall interest coverage)	4.10X's
Gross profit margin	25.0%
Net profit margin	4.0%
Return on total assets	4.0%
Return on net worth	7.00%

[4]All ratios based on year-end (rather than average) figures and on 360 (rather than 365) days in a year.

Case 1

ABINGTON-HILL TOYS, INC.

(Part II: Financial Planning)

David Hartly, comptroller of AH, completed the financial analysis of the firm and, based upon his findings, suggested the following course of action:[1]

1. Seek a long-term loan such that the firm's long-term debt would be increased to a level of $386,000.

2. Take steps to make the following ratios conform to industry averages:

    a. average collection period

    b. inventory turnover

3. Reduce short-term notes payable to $30,000.

4. Sell plant and equipment with an original cost of $140,000 and accumulated depreciation of $65,000 for its book value of $75,000.

In his final report to the president, Hartly wanted to show the effect of the successful implementation of his plan on the financial condition of the firm. The plan could conceivably be fully implemented by the end of January if approved by the president.

---

[1]See Abington-Hill Toys, Inc., Part I.

QUESTIONS

1. Prepare a set of pro forma financial statements for the end of January reflecting Hartly's proposed plan. In preparing these statements, you may assume the following:

   a. Sales for 1977 are estimated to be $1,200,000 and January sales are equal to 1/12 of that amount.

   b. Variable expenses including cost of goods sold remain at a constant proportion of sales.

   c. Fixed operating expenses and depreciation for January are equal to 1/12 of the 1975 totals.

   d. Interest expense of $2,500 is incurred and paid in January.

   e. Accounts payable increase to $46,000 and accrued expenses remain constant at $24,000.

   f. Assume the January tax liability is paid during that month.

2. Using the pro forma balance sheet and income statement developed above, prepare a cash budget for the month of January.

3. Evaluate the financial condition of the firm after the successful implementation of Hartly's proposal. (A ratio analysis of the firm's pro forma statements for January 31, 1977 would be one way to assess the financial condition of the firm after implementing the plan.)

Case 1

ABINGTON-HILL TOYS, INC.

(Part III: Financial Planning)

Upon completion of his financial analysis of AH (see Abington Hill Toys, Inc., Part I), the company comptroller, David Hartly, concluded that the principal action to be taken immediately was to seek out a term loan whose proceeds could be used to repay $194,000 of the firm's short-term notes. The particular note in question is due in March of the coming year. Part of the needed funds is expected to come from operations and another portion from the sale of fixed assets during January for $75,000 (accumulated depreciation on the assets is $65,000, while the original purchase price was $140,000).

In addition to paying off the short-term note in March, Hartly feels that the firm should increase its cash balance to a minimum level of $40,000. Although he believes the firm should attempt to reach this cash balance goal as soon as possible, Hartly recognizes the fact that additional short-term loans would be prohibitively expensive (factoring of accounts receivable or an inventory loan is possible but would cost an estimated 20 percent per annum). Thus, Hartly hopes to be able to hold out with the firm's existing cash balance ($10,000), plus cash flow from operations, until March, when he intends to seek the long-term loan. The proceeds from the loan in conjunction with funds from operations will be used to clear up $194,000 in notes payable and reach the desired cash balance of $40,000.

Sales estimates for the next seven months, as well as past monthly sales for the previous three months, are presented in Exhibit 1.

EXHIBIT 1

Abington-Hill Toys, Inc.

Sales Data

1976		1977	
October	$100,000	January	$90,000
November	$100,000	February	$90,000
December	$150,000	March	$90,000
		April	$100,000
		May	$110,000
		June	$100,000
		July	$90,000

Traditionally, AH's sales have been 60 percent credit and 40 percent cash. Of the credit sales, roughly half are collected one month after the sale and the remainder collected two months after the sale with negligible bad debt losses. Purchases are approximately 75 percent of sales and are made one month in advance, with payment following in 60 days. Variable cash operating expenses (including selling costs, wages, advertising, and miscellaneous cash expenses) are 7 percent of sales and are paid in the month in which they are incurred. Fixed cash operating expenses are roughly $2,500 a month, with payment made in the same month. Taxes are paid quarterly (April for the quarter ended in March, and so on) based on estimated earnings for the quarter. Annual depreciation expense is $60,000 on the net assets remaining after the January 1, 1977 sale of fixed assets. Interest expense for the notes payable is 12 percent and is payable quarterly in March and June. Interest on the outstanding long-term debt is at a rate of 6.06 percent and is paid semiannually in June and December. The term loan is expected to carry a 9.5 percent rate of interest, with interest payable semiannually beginning in September and the entire principal amount due in five years.

QUESTIONS

1. Based on the information provided, prepare a cash budget for AH covering the first quarter of 1977.
2. Based on your answers to question 1, how much should AH seek in additional long-term debt to pay off the $194,000 note and increase cash to a level of $40,000?
3. Prepare a cash budget for the second quarter of 1977. You may assume that AH was successful in renegotiating its line of credit with its bank carrying a $100,000 line and an 8.5 percent rate of interest with interest paid monthly.
4. Based on your answers to the preceding questions, prepare a pro forma income statement and balance sheet as of the end of the six-month budget period.

Case 2

GOLDEN BUFFALO
SKI WEAR

(Financial Ratio Analysis)

In September 1975, Calvin Duncan, a recent MBA graduate, was hired as a loan-lending officer for Washington State American Bank. Duncan graduated with honors and had previous experience working at the bank during the past three summers. One of his first assignments in his new position was to review the account of Golden Buffalo Ski Wear (GBSW), a long-standing client of the bank. GBSW had recently applied for an increase in their line of credit from $3 to $4 million and also requested a 10-year extension on a $2 million bank loan issued 10 years ago and due in October 1976.

Duncan's initial approach to the problem was to do some research into the background of the company. He found that GBSW was formed in 1934 by Andrew Todd, a man then in his mid-40s who was making his first attempt at owning and operating his own business. GBSW specialized in the manufacture and sale of a line of sophisticated, high quality ski sweaters. The company had remained quite small until the ski industry boom in the 1960s. Then, along with an increased interest in skiing, GBSW's sales grew steadily, going from $4.3 million in 1960, to $9.2 million in 1965, $20.1 million in 1970, and $25.7 million in 1975. Of these approximately 70 percent were credit sales.

Until 1970, GBSW had been owned and operated by the Todd family, with James Todd taking over for his father in 1950. James Todd was quite proud of the fact that under his management, although he kept within the guidelines originally set by his father, GBSW was realizing tremendous growth in sales and profits. Upon his retirement in 1970, GBSW was sold two times within the next year—first to a group of Chicago businessmen and then to a syndicate of Denver businessmen headed by James Gentry, thus ending the 36-year Todd control of the firm.

The Todd family had been quite conservative in their management of GBSW, limiting the product line to high quality ski sweaters sold only in ski shops and specially approved men's wear stores, but the Gentry syndicate took a more aggressive approach. They expanded the product line to include ski pants, ski jackets, shirts, and high fashion sweaters, drastically expanding the number of type of sales outlets to include department stores and some chain discount stores. This expansion in product line was financed in large part through the issuance of $7.5 million of 10 percent long-term debt in October 1974. This debt was due in 15 years (1990), and carried an annual sinking fund provision of $500,000, with the first sinking fund payment being made one year after the bonds were issued. Aside from the $2 million bank loan due in June 1976, this was the first long-term debt that GBSW had employed, previously limiting the capital structure to common and preferred stocks. The Gentry syndicate was hoping that this aggressive expansion, relying heavily on the good name of GBSW, would help to recapture the company's growth recorded in the 1960s.

Duncan further found that the preferred stock outstanding is nonparticipating and has a cumulative feature. This means that while the preferred stockholders cannot participate in the residual earnings of the firm, any unpaid dividends to preferred stockholders are carried forward and must be fully paid off before any dividends to common stockholders can be paid. In addition, preferred stockholders are allowed to elect one-half of the board of directors in the case of a dividend default, where arrearages on two quarterly dividend payments constitutes a default. Thus, the management of GBSW has no intention of even passing up a preferred dividend. The common stock is currently selling at around $40 per share and is paying $1.50 in annual dividends, with the dividends growing at about 10 percent per year. GBSW had not missed or lowered its annual divided payment in over 10 years and as such had become a favorite of pension and trust funds, which has resulted in a relatively stable stock price.

For the past four years Washington State American Bank has granted GBSW a line of credit for $3 million. The need for seasonal borrowing for GBSW is a result of its highly seasonal sales pattern and limited production facilities. Throughout the year GBSW is forced to keep production near full capacity, building large inventories that will be reduced from mid-July through December when 90 percent of the sales take place. Thus, for GBSW, short-term borrowing generally reaches a peak in August and is completely repaid by the end of November. While they have had a line of credit of $3 mililon for the past four years, the company's high credit was only for $2.6 million in August 1974.

In preparing his report for Washington State American Bank, Duncan will be required to prepare a sources and uses of funds statements for the past two years, to provide some insight into how GBSW has used its funds in the past. A complete ratio analysis of the firm, focusing on liquidity, debt, coverage, and profitability ratios, also will be necessary. In addition to the calculations of these ratios and an analysis of them, a tentative recommendation on both the line of credit and the loan extension is required by Duncan. This analysis will be based upon the financial data given in Exhibits 1, 2, and 3.

EXHIBIT 1

Golden Buffalo Ski Wear

Balance Sheet
As of August 31, 1973-75
(in $1,000s)

Assets		1973		1974		1975
Cash		$ 2,100		$ 1,800		$ 1,600
Accounts receivable		1,400		1,800		1,500
Raw materials & supplies	800		1,000		1,200	
Work in process	2,600		3,500		4,600	
Finished goods	200		300		500	
Inventory		3,600		4,800		6,300
Total current assets		7,100		8,400		9,400
Fixed assets at cost	22,900		27,000		34,500	
Less: accumulated depreciation	6,300		6,600		6,900	
Net fixed assets		16,600		20,400		27,600
Goodwill		12,000		12,000		12,000
Total assets		35,700		40,800		49,000
Liabilities						
Line of credit		2,400		2,600		2,400
Accounts payable		700		1,000		1,600
Accruals		300		500		800
Total current liabilities		3,400		4,100		4,800
Bank loan (due Oct. 1976)		2,000		2,000		2,000
Long-term debt		-		-		7,500
Preferred stock[1]		12,000		12,000		12,000
Common stock[2]		4,000		5,000		5,000
Paid-in surplus		10,000		13,000		13,000
Retained earnings		4,300		4,700		4,700
Total stockholders' equity		30,300		34,700		34,700
Total liabilities & equity		35,700		40,800		49,000

[1]On August 31, 1975 there were 625,000 shares of common outstanding.
[2]On August 31, 1975 there were 120,000 shares of preferred stock outstanding with a par value of $100 each and yielding 7.5 percent.

EXHIBIT 2

Golden Buffalo Ski Wear

Income Statements for the Years Ending
August 31, 1973 through 1975
(in $1,000s)

	1973	1974	1975
Net sales	$20,600	$24,200	$25,700
Cost of goods sold	14,700	17,300	18,400
Gross profit	5,900	6,900	7,300
Selling general & administrative expenses	993	1,828	2,233
Depreciation	650	650	650
Earnings before interest & taxes	4,257	4,422	4,417
Interest expense	200	200	950
Earnings before taxes	4,057	4,222	3,467
Taxes	1,907	1,984.5	1,629.5
Net profit after tax	2,150	2,237.5	1,837.5
Dividends paid:			
Common	750.	937.5	937.5
Preferred	900.	900.	900.

EXHIBIT 3

Industry Averages For
Selected Ratios (1973-75)

Ratio	Average
Current ratio	1.943
Acid test ratio	.969
Average collection period ratio	40.3 days
Inventory turnover ratio	3.877 times
Total debt to net worth	.636
Long-term debt to total capitalization	.487
Gross profit margin	23.4%
Net profit margin	9.64%
Asset turnover ratio	.826 times
Return on assets (earning power)	7.96%
Interest coverage ratio	4.533 times

QUESTIONS

1. Calculate the following financial ratios for Golden Buffalo Ski Wear for 1973, '74 and '75.

   Current ratio
   Acid test ratio
   Average collection period ratio[1]
   Inventory turnover ratio[2]
   Total debt to net worth
   Long-term debt to total capitalization
   Gross profit margin
   Net profit margin
   Tangible asset turnover ratio
   Return on tangible assets ratio (earning power ratio)
   Interest coverage ratio

2. Comment on the strengths and weaknesses uncovered by this analysis.

3. If a value for annual cash flow before interest and taxes was available, what other coverage ratio might be useful? Why is this ratio somewhat more meaningful than the simple interest coverage ratio?

4. Assuming that a value for annual cash flow before interest and taxes is not available, how might the simple interest coverage ratio be modified to examine coverage of other fixed charges for GBSW? What does this analysis indicate? (Use 50 percent as the federal tax rate.)

5. Prepare a sources and uses of funds statement for GBSW for 1974 and 1975. What is the purpose of this analysis?

6. Prepare a percentage income statement for GBSW for 1974 and 1975. What is the purpose of this analysis?

7. If you were Calvin Duncan, what would be your recommendation as to Golden Buffalo's request for an extension and increase in their line of credit and refinancing of their $2 million of long-term debt? Why?

[1] Use year-end receivables as average receivables.

[2] Use the value for ending inventory as given on the balance sheet as a surrogate for average inventory.

Case 3

PHIFER DRUG CORPORATION

(Financial Ratio Analysis)

In the recent past the ethical drug industry has prospered. While numerous other industries faced financial difficulties in the 1974-75 recessionary period, most ethical drug firms never broke stride. The sales volume of the majority of these corporations continued to grow steadily. However, despite such overall favorable results within the industry Bernard O'Laughlin, president of Phifer Drug Corporation, has been anything but pleased with the financial picture of his organization. Although O'Laughlin is relieved to see a recovery from the downturn in sales encountered by his firm in 1974, he remains quite concerned about the profitability being generated from these sales. The firm has maintained a profitable status, but one of O'Laughlin's primary questions relates to the adequacy of the profits. On several occasions, he has confronted his vice president, George Melton, with such concerns. However, to date O'Laughlin does not consider his questions to have been satisfactorily resolved. In response to his inquiries, Melton notes that the firm's operating profits have increased by a "staggering 141 percent" within the last four years. From this fact, Melton is convinced that the company's financial condition has improved in an impressive fashion. As additional supporting data for his conviction of the corporation's overall prosperity, Melton cites the fact that Phifer's cost of production has consistently been less than half the dollar sales for its products.

In spite of Melton's conclusion that the firm is doing adequately well, O'Laughlin continues to desire more specific financial information relating to the strengths and weaknesses of Phifer Drug Corporation. In this regard, he has acquired the financial data of Phifer's principal competitor, Moreau-Pasche, Inc. O'Laughlin has for some time felt the competitive pressure from this organiza-tion. Hence, he believes an analysis making an in-depth comparison of the two business entities would specifically explain whether or not his dissatisfaction is justified. Although O'Laughlin has not had an opportunity to do a complete investigation, he has computed the return on assets (on a before-tax basis) for Moreau-Pasche and found it to be significantly higher than the equivalent figure for Phifer. Furthermore, he has noticed his institution's earnings per share to be less than the same computation for Moreau-Pasche in 1976. On the other hand, he did take some comfort in discovering Phifer's return-on-common to be some-what closer to Moreau-Pasche than the return-on-assets. Also, O'Laughlin made a point to compute his competitor's growth in operating income during the most recent four-year period, which proved to be less than the comparable growth rate for Phifer. Since he had not performed a thorough examination, he could not definitely explain the reasons for the more narrow margin between the two firm's return on common and Phifer's larger growth rate in operating income; however, he thought it to be the result of recent investment decisions and Phifer's dividend policy.

In a recent meeting with the   company's financial officer, O'Laughlin enumerated his concerns as being:

1. Is the business maintaining an adequate liquidity position?
2. Is the management of Phifer Corporation generating sufficient return on the firm's operating assets on a before-tax basis?
3. Does the financial mix appear to be appropriate?
4. Is an ample return on common being provided to attract future common stockholders? In this particular matter, O'Laughlin is especially interested in knowing the key variables having an impact upon the return on common.

CASE REQUIREMENTS

1. Perform a financial-ratio analysis that gives detailed attention to O'Laugh-lin's four questions. Conduct your investigation in terms of both time (the five years given) and relative to Moreau-Pasche. Where relevant, use a 365-day year in your computations.
2. Make recommendations to O'Laughlin with respect to any financial matters needing attention.
3. Evaluate both O'Laughlin's and Melton's beliefs about the financial position of the company.

EXHIBIT 1

Phifer Corporation

Income Statements for 1972-1976

	1972	1973	1974	1975	1976
Sales[1]	$ 7,053	$ 8,301	$ 7,694	$ 8,806	$ 10,046
Cost of goods sold	3,455	3,968	3,526	4,115	4,823
Gross profit	3,598	4,333	4,168	4,691	5,223
Operating expenses[2]					
General and administrative	2,380	2,499	2,221	2,471	3,033
Selling and advertising	274	307	371	460	353
Depreciation	156	183	174	195	205
Research and development	298	330	354	397	449
Total operating expenses	3,108	3,319	3,120	3,523	4,040
Operating income	490	1,014	1,048	1,168	1,183
Other income[3]	154	158	172	173	216
Earnings before interest and taxes	644	1,172	1,220	1,341	1,399
Interest expense	122	140	161	186	253
Earnings before taxes	522	1,032	1,059	1,155	1,146
Income taxes (40%)	209	413	424	462	458
Earnings after taxes	313	619	635	693	688
Preferred dividends	31	0	0	0	0
Earnings available for common	282	619	635	693	688
Common dividends	258	320	334	350	370
Increase in retained earnings	$ 24	$ 299	$ 301	$ 343	$ 318
Earnings per share	$ .82	$ 1.40	$ 1.41	$ 1.52	$ 1.45
Number of common shares	344,803	440,625	451,430	455,250	474,485

[1]Credit sales normally comprise 80 percent of total sales.

[2]Lease payments included in the operational expenses are $100,000 in 1972 and 1973, $200,000 in 1974 and 1975, and $400,000 in 1976.

[3]Other income is made up of profits from Hawkins Industries, a Phifer subsidiary in the cosmetics industry, and long-term security investments.

EXHIBIT 2

Phifer Corporation

Balance Sheets for December 31, 1972-1976 ($000)

	1972	1973	1974	1975	1976
Current assets					
Cash and equivalent	$ 449	$ 484	$ 559	$1,223	$ 1,373
Accounts receivable[1]	1,206	1,519	1,840	2,017	2,239
Inventories[1]	1,253	1,570	1,419	1,670	2,218
Other current assets	123	133	438	252	325
Total current assets	$3,031	$3,706	$4,296	$5,162	$ 6,155
Fixed assets					
Gross plant	$3,811	$4,536	$4,465	$4,790	$ 5,206
Reserve for depreciation	1,522	1,675	1,574	1,694	1,778
Net plant and equipment	$2,289	$2,861	$2,889	$3,096	$ 3,428
Intangible assets	493	594	546	575	564
Other assets					
Investments in subsidiaries	45	50	41	45	40
Investments - other	445	565	856	719	510
Miscellaneous assets	18	27	41	43	48
Total other assets	508	643	939	807	598
Total assets	$6,321	$7,804	$8,670	$9,640	$10,745
Liabilities					
Current liabilities	$1,450	$1,687	$1,942	$1,987	$ 2,326
Long-term debt[2]	1,196	1,543	1,623	1,992	2,251
Deferred taxes	123	141	243	242	240
Other liabilities	100	122	141	166	189
Total liabilities	$2,869	$3,493	$3,949	$4,387	$ 5,006
Net worth:					
Preferred stock	1,028	0	0	0	0
Common equity	1,931	3,717	4,175	5,678	5,175
Total net worth	3,452	4,311	4,721	5,253	5,740
Total liabilities and net worth	$6,321	$7,804	$8,670	$9,640	$10,745

[1] Beginning accounts receivable and inventory balances for 1972 were $1,000,000 and $1,100,000, respectively. Also, with respect to the receivables, the policy of the firm is to extend credit for 60 days on credit sales.

[2] The indenture of the long-term debt places a 10 percent sinking fund requirement upon the firm.

EXHIBIT 3

Moreau-Pasche, Inc.

Income Statements for 1972-1976

	1972	1973	1974	1975	1976
Sales[1]	$ 3,912	$ 4,368	$ 5,042	$ 6,116	$ 7,038
Cost of goods sold	1,093	1,199	1,168	1,447	1,726
Gross profit	2,819	3,169	3,874	4,669	5,312
Operating expenses[2]					
General and administrative	1,184	1,346	1,574	1,885	2,222
Selling and advertising	380	400	519	606	651
Depreciation	83	80	116	132	147
Research and development	214	252	286	300	371
Total operating expenses	1,861	2,078	2,495	2,923	3,391
Operating income	958	1,091	1,379	1,746	1,921
Other income[3]	0	11	27	35	64
Earnings before interest and taxes	958	1,102	1,406	1,781	1,985
Interest expense	10	12	15	20	33
Earnings before taxes	948	1,090	1,391	1,761	1,952
Income taxes (40%)	379	436	556	704	781
Earnings after taxes	569	654	835	1,057	1,171
Preferred dividends	12	11	6	3	2
Earnings available for common	557	643	829	1,054	1,169
Common dividends	176	222	243	291	407
Increase in retained earnings	$ 381	$ 421	$ 586	$ 763	$ 762
Earnings per share	$ .72	$ .82	$ 1.05	$ 1.33	$ 1.47
Number of common shares	775,000	580,250	788,500	790,500	593,240

[1]Credit sales normally represent 90 percent of total sales.

[2]No lease payments are incurred.

[3]Other income is provided from a relatively small investment in short-term securities and a 1976 investment in long-term securities.

EXHIBIT 4

Moreau-Pasche, Inc.

Balance Sheets for December 31, 1972-1976

	1972	1973	1974	1975	1976
Current Assets					
Cash and equivalent	$ 627	$ 960	$1,453	$1,800	$1,171
Accounts receivable[1]	714	745	807	988	1,229
Inventories[1]	656	633	735	867	1,515
Other current assets	225	280	317	382	444
Total current assets	2,222	2,618	3,312	4,037	4,359
Fixed Assets					
Gross plant	1,352	1,608	1,822	2,183	2,780
Less depreciation	502	566	640	733	846
Net plant and equipment	850	1,042	1,182	1,450	1,934
Intangible Assets	121	123	98	102	122
Other Assets					
Investments	0	0	0	74	174
Total Assets	$3,193	$3,783	$4,592	$5,663	$6,589
Liabilities					
Current liabilities	$ 700	$ 795	$1,010	$1,290	$1,493
Long-term debt	38	131	128	83	7
Deferred taxes	12	11	12	16	53
Other liabilities	56	74	92	110	0
Total liabilities	806	1,011	1,242	1,499	1,553
Subordinated preferred stock	17	18	22	26	35
Net Worth:					
Preferred stock	241	206	90	21	0
Common equity	2,008	2,425	3,140	4,015	4,879
Intangibles	121	123	98	102	122
Total net worth	$2,370	$2,754	$3,328	$4,138	$5,001
Total liabilities and net worth	$3,193	$3,783	$4,592	$5,663	$6,589

[1] Beginning accounts receivable and inventory balances for 1972 were $700,000 and $600,000, respectively.

Case 4

TIGER POOL SALES

(Cash Budgeting)

In mid-March, H. Huckleby, president of Tiger Pool Sales (TPS) contacted Financial Advisors, Inc. to arrange for a professional consultant to come into his company. In the past year it had become increasingly evident that TPS was having definite problems in formulating their cash flows. On March 31 Financial Advisors sent over Jackie Lynn. It was planned that she would work with TPS for a one month period to help them analyze their cash inflows and outflows, and thereby more efficiently manage their cash budget. Lynn spent her first week working closely with Huckleby learning company background and basic operational strategies. She set her first goal as the formulation of a cash budget covering the next six months.

During her first week with the company, Lynn learned that TPS was founded in 1954 by Huckleby as a pool construction firm based in Woodridge, Illinois. It was a small business that grew quite rapidly, surrounded as it was by some of the wealthier counties in northern Illinois.

Although TPS had shown good growth and profit-making ability in the past, it always had been faced with considerable cash flow problems resulting from its highly seasonal sales pattern. As a result, in 1973, in an attempt to reduce this seasonal trend, TPS set up winter operations in Merritt Island, Florida. Although this effort did have a stabilizing effect on the monthly sales pattern, it did not eliminate the problem, since, as of 1975, Illinois sales remained three times greater than Florida sales.

In July 1974, cash flow problems caused by this seasonal pattern of sales forced the postponement of the purchase of some badly needed construction equipment, which resulted in long construction delays. As a result TPS was forced to take a five-year loan of $200,000 at 10 percent per annum at the First American Bank of Woodridge.

In September 1974, in an attempt to speed up TPS's cash flows, James William, bookkeeper for TPS, contacted Mainline Billing Inc., to handle billing and aid in the collection of deliquent accounts. This resulted in a significant improvement in average collection time primarily in those accounts over one month past due. William reported to Huckleby that currently 10 percent of the sales were for cash, 20 percent were being paid within 30 days after the sale, an additional 7 percent of the credit sales was being paid for 90 days after the sale, and 3 percent of all credit sales resulted in bad debts. Although instituting this new billing system for customers and developing tighter credit checks and collection procedures did not alleviate TPS's total problem, it did bring about significant improvement in its average collection period and bad debts to total sales ratios. William has also approached Huckleby with the possibility of offering trade discounts to customers as a method of speeding up collection of accounts receivable. This alternative has been seriously considered by Huckleby, but it has not been adopted because, as Huckleby says, "Why should we bribe customers to pay their bills on time when that is what they are legally obligated to do anyway? The whole idea sounds shady, costs money, and doesn't make much sense." The actual sales through March 1975 and the forecasted sales for the following six months are given in Exhibit 1.

EXHIBIT 1

Actual and Expected Sales
1st 9 months - 1975

	$	15,000
		10,000
		25,000
		30,000
		60,000
		100,000
		100,000
		60,000
		25,000

In looking at TPS's cash flow patterns, Lynn found that the cash outflows are largely tied to expected future sales, with expenditures on cost of goods sold amounting to 60 percent of the following month's sales. In addition, TPS pays wages and salaries amounting to $5,000 per month plus variable wages, resulting from unskilled labor hired to help in peak seasons. Expected variable wages are given in Exhibit 2. The sales and administrative expenses are $10,000 per month plus 5 percent of the current monthly sales. TPS's rent

EXHIBIT 2

Expected Variable Wages

April	$ 1,000
May	3,000
June	6,000
July	6,000
August	3,000
September	1,000

expenditures are constant over the year, running approximately $2,000 per month. Moreover, a semiannual interest payment on the $200,000, 6 percent loan from First American Bank is due in July along with the first sinking fund payment on that loan of $40,000. Along with these cash outflows, a dividend payment of $10,000 is expected to be declared in May and made during the coming June; while tax payments of $5,000 are to be made on the calendar quarters. In addition, the capital expenditure associated with the construction equipment that had originally been planned for purchase in 1974 was postponed until May of 1975 and would involve $30,000. One third of this expenditure will be paid for immediately in cash, with the second third being paid for in June and the remaining portion in September. The final expense incurred by TPS during this planning period is monthly depreciation of $3,000.

Through discussions with Huckleby, Lynn learned that TPS always carries a minimum cash balance of $25,000 on hand. Huckleby feels that any less would interfere with TPS's ability to conduct its ordinary business, that is, making purchases and sales, given the unpredictability of cash inflows and outflows. On March 31, 1975, this cash balance was $5,000 above the minimum at $30,000, and on April 31, 1975, Lynn's cash budget was due.

QUESTIONS

1. If Tiger Pool Sales can estimate their profit in the upcoming months, is it necessary for them also to estimate their cash budget? Why?

2. What time period (monthly, daily, hourly) should we attempt to analyze in preparing a cash budget?

3. Prepare a cash budget for April through September.

4. If inflows and outflows are not constant during each month, might the analysis be affected?

5. What was the most important estimate required in making this analysis? Why?

6. Comment on Huckleby's opinion of trade credit discounts.

7. What should be the cash strategy that Jackie Lynn recommends to Huckleby?

Case 5

HARLINGTON MANUFACTURING COMPANY

(Cash Budgeting)

In July 1976, Jim Hunter purchased the Harlington Manufacturing Company for $200,000. Hunter is 48 years old and was vice-president with a large manufacturing firm prior to his acquisition of Harlington. Although he had been very successful, he had long dreamed of having his own business and settling down to a less hectic life-style. The opportunity to purchase Harlington came suddenly, and Hunter was quick to recognize the opportunity as a sound one.

Hunter's industrial experience was primarily in marketing and sales; however, he had some limited contact with the financial aspects of a firm's management. Harlington's primary problem at the time of acquisition related to the rather loose control exercised by its former owner, who had been trying to sell the firm and retire for the past four years. During the first five months of his management, Hunter was able to reduce operating costs substantially and in general "tighten up" the firm's operations. This reorganization resulted in some minor personnel changes, but primarily took the form of better control over production scheduling, materials management, and direct labor cost.

Although significant improvements had been made in the firm's overall operations, Hunter felt that his decisions could best be characterized as "seat of the pants," and he wanted to implement a better system for planning future expenditures. In the past the firm had utilized a very loosely constructed cash flow statement and depended on its line of credit with the Mercantile National

Bank for any cash deficiencies from operations.[1] Hunter believed that this system was simply inadequate in light of his plans for expansion of the firm's operations over the next two years.

Just before closing down the plant for a one-week period at Christmas, Hunter asked that his production and sales supervisors provide him with a complete set of monthly sales and expense estimates covering the first half of 1977. This information, along with the company's past operating history, was used to compile the predicted revenue and expense data found in Exhibit 1.

EXHIBIT 1

	Jan.	Feb.	Mar.	Apr.	May	June	July
Sales	$250,000.	260,000.	270,000.	260.000.	250,000.	250,000.	260,000.
Salaries	5,800.	5,800.	5,800.	5,800.	5,800.	5,800.	5,800.
Utilities	1,250.	1,250.	1,250.	1,250.	1,250.	1,250.	1,250.
Rent	1,200.	1,200.	1,200.	1,200.	1,200.	1,200.	1,200.
Advertising	500.	500.	500.	500.	500.	500.	500.
Depreciation	200.	200.	200.	200.	200.	200.	200.
Office Supplies[1]	450.	450.	450.	450.	450.	450.	450.

[1]Postage, stationary, coffee room supplies, and such.

In addition to those items included in Exhibit 1, Hunter was told that purchases were 75 percent of sales and were made one month in advance on credit terms of 1/15 net 60.[2] Also, direct labor cost (wages) are estimated at 10 percent of cost of sales with wages paid weekly. Finally, sales commissions amounted to 2 percent of sales and were paid one month following the month in which the sales occurred.

Beyond these operating revenue and expense items, the firm incurs a number of expenses related to overhead, loan repayments, interest, insurance, and dividends. The predicted amounts of these expenses for the next six months are shown in Exhibit 2.

After inquiring about the firm's collections, Hunter learned that approximately 60 percent of the firm's customers take advantage of the cash discount terms (1/15, net 60) offered by the firm, with another 10 percent paying within 30 days after the sale and 29 percent making payment during the second month after the sale. Bad debts are estimated at 1 percent of sales.

Hunter plans to embark on a major expansion as soon as the firm has

---

[1]Hunter had continued the good working relationship with the Mercantile National Bank and had arranged for a $50,000 line of credit at 1 percent over prime.

[2]The firm follows the practice of taking all cash discounts.

EXHIBIT 2

Amount	Date Due	Explanation
$ 1,000.	February	Last installment on two delivery vans purchased in 1976.
2,000.	March	Semiannual interest on long-term debt
400.	March and June	Common stock dividends[1]
1,000.	March	Payroll taxes
20,000.	January	Quarterly income tax payment
20,000.	April	Quarterly income tax payment
52,000.	April	Bank note due
650.	June	Semiannual insurance premium

[1] $.40 per share on 1,000 outstanding shares, all of which are held by Hunter.

generated sufficient funds internally. The expansion will require approximately $50,000 as an initial expenditure followed by a total outlay of $200,000 over the next two years. In light of the firm's past use of debt funds (primarily a $50,000 five-year note with an insurance company), Hunter feels that the initial outlay must come from internally generated funds.

QUESTIONS AND PROBLEMS

1. Based on the information provided, prepare a monthly cash budget for Harlington covering the next six months. Sales for November and December of 1976 were $250,000 and $270,000, respectively.

2. If Hunter believes that the firm should maintain a minimum cash balance of $5,000 and if the beginning balance for December is $6,000, identify the months and the amounts of funds that Harlington will have to borrow in the budget period. You may assume borrowing in minimum increments of $1,000 with interest payable at 12 percent per annum in the month for which the loan is outstanding. Repayments should be made as soon as sufficient funds are available. Also, excess cash can be invested for minimum periods of 90 days and in units of $10,000 to earn a net return of 8 percent (before taxes but after brokerage fees).

3. When approximately will the firm have sufficient funds available to make the down payment on the planned expansion?

Case 6

THE JACKSON FARM

(Part I: Cash Budgeting)

It was the day after the Thanksgiving holiday, and Howard Jackson was a contented man. He had just finished an early, country-style breakfast with his wife and two sons. Both boys, only a year apart in age, were home from college until Monday; during this period they enjoyed taking over the operation of the farm. This gave Jackson some "time away from the fields." He used this pause to attend to bookkeeping matters, and he did so with a great attention to detail. This business attribute was unlike that possessed by many of his neighbors, who owned and lived by the running of similar farms.

Jackson settled into the comfortable den of his large farmhouse, and lit the logs that rested in the stone-faced fireplace. The den faced directly the sharp winds that blew east over the foothills of the Allegheny Mountains. He wanted to remove the chill that pervaded the den during the morning hours.

Running this farm is a pleasure for Jackson. Three years ago he had effected a major career change, which at the time appeared to be drastic but to him was more of a dream. He is now 45 years old. Prior to the purchase of his 540-acre farm near Monterey, Virginia, Jackson had put in exactly 20 years with Bethard-Wheeling Iron and Steel. Those years saw him rise from the position of cost clerk to that of director of cost accounting systems for the entire firm. While with Bethard-Wheeling, Jackson occupied positions in the four-state region of Pennsylvania, West Virginia, Virginia, and Maryland.

Three events occurred almost simultaneously that resulted in his leaving the post with the steel manufacturer and entering the agribusiness industry. First, Jackson suffered a slight coronary warning, as it was described by his physician. Although no actual damage affected the heart muscle, Sally Jackson (his wife) strongly suggested that the sometimes strong demands of his executive position (which regularly translated into 16-to-18-hour workdays) had taken an unreasonable toll on his physical condition. Second, the fact that Jackson had served Bethard-Wheeling for 20 years meant that he could retire and draw immediate pension benefits. The vesting provisions of the pension plan, run privately by this manufacturer, were among the more liberal in the steel industry. The requirement for a fully vested right in the pension plan was that the worker's age plus years of work service total 62. Howard had reached that milestone at such a relatively young age (then 42) because he had not switched employers during his career within the Financial Controls Department of Bethard-Wheeling. Upon retirement, he began drawing (on a monthly basis) annual benefits totaling exactly 55 percent of the average of his last 5 years' annual salary. That turned out to be 55 percent of $38,000. The third situation that prompted Jackson's leaving the world of manufacturing was the opportunity to purchase, through an estate auction, the farmland and operation he now managed.

Located in east-central Virginia, The Jackson Farm (TJF) consists primarily of 540 acres of open, fertile, limestone-based land, a few wooded acres, plus several buildings. Jackson was especially concerned on this day after Thanksgiving with the preparation of an estimate of cash receipts and disbursements covering the upcoming year for TJF. A 150-acre parcel of land that he especially prized was to be put on the market in January. The land lay adjacent to his present operation and would be easy to mold into the overall activities of the farm. Jackson knew that he could not pay cash for the 150-acre parcel, but had discussed a real estate loan with the credit analyst at the Farmers' Loan Association. As one piece of information to evaluate, the credit analyst requested that Jackson prepare a formal cash budget to cover the next January-December period of operations. Jackson turned to this task, which he did regularly each year at this time, but not in quite the detail that would characterize the present budget.

The heart of TJF is its herd of Hereford cattle. One-hundred brooder cows are owned. These cows (recognizable by their white face, reddish coat, and white markings) have produced, on the average, one calf each per year. Last week Jackson purchased 50 feeder calves. These calves individually weighed about 380 to 420 pounds and cost an average of $140. Payment for the calves will occur at the rate of one-third of the total price during each of the first three months of next year. Also, at this time next year another 40 feeder calves will be acquired, but the first payment will occur during December, with the remaining two of the three equal payments taking place in January and February of the budget period subsequent to this one. The estimated price of the calves next year is placed at a lower level of $132 per animal.

All of the feeders acquired last week combined with 88 of the calves reared from the brooder herd will be sold within the cash planning period. These

138 yearlings will weigh in the neighborhood of 750 to 900 pounds each. The projected selling price is an average of $290 per head. The timing of the sales is noted in Exhibit 1.

EXHIBIT 1

The Jackson Farm

Sale of Yearlings

Month	Number to be Sold
April	28
July	41
September	41
October	28

The terms of sale for the yearlings is 10 percent cash down and 90 percent to be received in the month following sale. At present, none of the brooder herd is unproductive, so no older cows will be marketed. Jackson realizes in future years, however, that some feeder calves might have to be retained and a few older cows sold to maintain an acceptable rate of production.

Another central facet of TJF is its sheep herd, which consists of 90 ewes. These livestock produce offspring at a normal annual rate of 130 percent per sheep. Jackson believes that the market for the lambs will bring $52 for each animal. The number of lambs sold during specific months has varied quite a bit in the past three years for TJF. Jackson reviewed his ledgers and settled upon the data displayed in Exhibit 2 as a reasonable estimate of the market liquidation pace for next year's lamb flock.

EXHIBIT 2

The Jackson Farm

Sale of Lambs

Month	Percent to be Sold
May	26
June	40
July	17
August	17

Full payment for the lambs would be received in the month immediately following the sale.

A by-product of raising sheep is the sheared wool available from the flock.

Jackson is forecasting that 650 pounds of wool will be sheared next spring. Although he is rather certain of the amount of wool that can be sold, the price at which it can be marketed is subject to more variability. Recalling (1) what he had received per pound in the past, (2) what his neighboring farm owners had received, and (3) his recent discussion with an agricultural extension agent from a major state university, some price estimates and their related chances of occurring (Exhibit 3) were put together. Half of the wool will be sold for cash in May and the other half in June. After some deliberation, Jackson decided to weigh all possible sales prices for the wool by their respective chances of occurring and use the resultant expected value as the price per pound in his final budget presentation. Further, as the price of wool this year was depressed below a subsidy level computed by the Agricultural Conservation Service, TJF would receive a cash payment amounting to $170 in April.

EXHIBIT 3

The Jackson Farm

Estimated Wool Prices

Possible Price Per Pound ($)	Probability of Occurrence
.33	.05
.34	.10
.35	.15
.36	.20
.38	.20
.39	.15
.40	.10
.41	.05

Jackson now reflected on deriving useful projections for payments arising from the purchase of feed, seed, and fertilizer. These sources of farm operating expense are highly certain as to their timing, but rising prices for all these items in recent years make estimation of the cost levels somewhat hazy. Continued prospects of this inflationary spiral removed part of the pleasant tinge that had previously engulfed Howard Jackson throughout preparation of the budget. During the current year, $1,800 would be spent on the acquisition of feed for the livestock possessed by TJF. Jackson felt that this would rise to $2,000 over the next planning period. The feed purchases will be of equal amounts concentrated into the (1) January through May and (2) October through December months of each year. Cash outflows for these eight payments would be made in the same month that the feed was acquired.

Besides selling cattle, sheep, and wool, TJF also benefits from the sale of grain. The grain is raised mainly to feed the livestock, but because of the size of the farm and its fertile land, some excess is always available for market. Oats and corn are regularly planted. The seeds for these crops will cost $720 in total and will be purchased in the middle of March. Payment will occur 30 days later. When the grain is harvested, another expense results. Both because of the high cost of harvesting equipment and the fact that he only uses such machinery twice a year, Jackson rents the equipment when it is needed. The oats are combined during July, the corn is harvested in October. The equipment is hired on a cash basis and will cost $220 for each rental. Based upon recent experience, Jackson believes that $1,500 can be received from the sale of excess oats. This surplus will be sold in July, with payment being received in August. From the current season, some $4,000 worth of "extra" corn is available. Half of this will be sold within two weeks (during December) and the other half during January. Cash receipts from the corn sale will occur in the month immediately following the sale. Next year, Jackson plans to accelerate the pace of liquidation of his surplus corn crop. Three years of operating TJF has provided him with enough confidence to estimate accurately the feed requirements of his cattle and sheep herds. Thus, the corn above his own forecasted needs will be sold in equal amounts upon harvest in October and during the month of November, about a year from now. Jackson estimates the value of the subsequent corn crop will be the same as this year's, and payment will follow the existing pattern.

Jackson recognizes well the benefits of effective fertilization of the corn crop. He anticipates spending $1,300 for such purposes during the one-year planning horizon. Plow down fertilizer amounting to $540 would be purchased in May. In July he would buy $760 worth of liquid nitrate and some herbicide. The terms of sale for these materials are 30 days net. On such terms it was Jackson's policy to delay payment until the very last day; therefore, the actual cash drain occurred in the month after receipt of the goods.

TJF employs part-time laborers on a continual basis to operate effectively. The average monthly labor expense has been in the area of $1,000 to $1,100. Jackson decided to play it safe on this input to the budget and chose the upper limit of this historical range to use as the projected monthly labor expense. In addition to this figure, a seasonal variation affects the labor cost estimates. Extra help has to be taken on during hay season to speed up the harvest and mitigate risk caused by the natural elements. TJF makes two-thirds of its hay in June, one-sixth in May, and one-sixth in July. The total added labor cost during hay season is projected to be $600. All labor is paid on a weekly basis.

Because of the rather random nature of their occurrence, Jackson decided to allocate evenly to each month of the year one-twelfth of the annual expected total of four categories of cash expenses. These items are (1) gas and oil, (2) veterinary services and medicine, (3) miscellaneous supplies, and (4) building and machinery repairs. The totals forecast for these expenditure sources are tabulated in Exhibit 4.

EXHIBIT 4

The Jackson Farm

Randomly Occurring Cash Expenditures

Source	Annual Outflow ($)
Gas and oil	1,400
Veterinary services and medicine	800
Miscellaneous supplies	500
Repairs	1,800

Other areas of expenditure that regularly draw upon the cash resources of TJF and have to be considered are: (1) its monthly interest and principal payment of $600, (2) a $2,000 county real estate tax paid every November, and (3) insurance payments of $300 each March and November. While pondering these noncontrollable outflows, Howard Jackson also noted that he would incur depreciation expense of $375 every month of the coming year.

Adding some stability to the revenue picture of TJF are the four, small, wood-frame houses located on each of the extreme corners of the farmland. Howard Jackson rents these houses, and because of his extraordinary attention to basic maintenance, has no trouble in finding local families willing to sign one-year leases in exchange for the right to rent and occupy the houses. As each of the houses is of about the same size, they rent for identical annual amounts of $1,560 each. Payment on these dwellings is received monthly.

A final source of income to TJF is the sale of firewood. Jackson has been clearing a few wooded acres on the farm and selling the preponderance of the wood at $25 per pick-up truck load, payable on delivery. During the next calendar year, he estimates 40 loads will be sold. The sales are forecast to occur in equal amounts in January, February, November, and December.

The current year has not been a good one for most cattle raisers. As a result, TJF will have no taxable income this year; thus, no tax payment will be built into the cash budget. Moreover, as the loss will be quite small for the current year, no tax refund resulting from the carryback procedure of net operating losses will be incorporated into the construction of the budget.

When the planning year begins, Howard Jackson will have a cash balance of $7,000 in his farm-related demand deposit account at a local bank. He uses a completely separate account for the personal needs of his family. For the most part, he is unconcerned with strict adherence to the maintenance of a minimum cash balance. This is because the local bank appreciates the demand deposit of TJF, and has informally (orally) agreed to a line of credit, not to exceed $5,000. which may be drawn down as needed. Because of a personal preference, however, Jackson dislikes the demand deposit balance of TJF to slip below $1,000. This $1,000 minimum cash level, then, will be a part of his formal budget.

PROBLEMS

1. Using all available information, construct a cash budget for The Jackson Farm covering the upcoming January-December period.

2. In your final budget package, include a schedule or financial worksheet that details by month the timing and amount of any necessary borrowing. Assume repayments on any needed borrowings are made as soon as cash is available for that purpose. Surplus funds will be accumulated as cash and not invested in any short-term financial assets. Further, the analyst from the Farmer's Loan Association has instructed Jackson to ignore inclusion of interest payments in the final budget schedules that may arise from any short-term borrowing.

3. As a secondary consideration, review your budget schedules and comment upon whether you think Jackson's commercial bank will be wary of, or highly concerned with, the financial position of the farm after the 12-month planning period has ended.

Case 6

THE JACKSON FARM

(Part II: Financial Ratio Analysis)

On this ninth day of January, Eliot Dudley finished his morning coffee at the small diner located in the center of the business district of Verona, Virginia. He then began to walk briskly the four blocks to his office. He was anticipating receiving some documents in today's mail that would permit him to take action on a real estate loan request made by Howard Jackson.

Dudley is the manager of the regional Farmers' Loan Association located in Verona. As manager, he serves as executive officer of this local association, a post he has occupied for the past 12 years. The Verona Farmers' Loan Association is regulated by the Federal Land Bank of Hagerstown, Maryland. The Maryland District consists of the five-state region encompassing Delaware, Maryland, Pennsylvania, Virginia, and West Virginia. Each regional association is actually a corporation, is organized by borrowers from its district, and is operated in a specifically defined geographic area under a federal charter. The local associations perform the critical function of originating business for the national Farm Credit System. By being close to the public, the local association is best able to determine the borrowing needs and capabilities of the farm businesses in its area. From a national perspective, the Federal Land Banks are a major supplier of real estate credit to agriculture. Dudley often speaks to local service clubs and groups as a vehicle for subtly advertising the financing services available through his association. Recently he has drawn upon the information shown in Exhibit 1 to point out that in terms of outstanding real estate debt, the Federal Land Banks are the largest institutional lender.

EXHIBIT 1

Farm Real Estate Debt Outstanding

Year-end Totals

Lender	1964		1974	
	Dollar Volume (in millions)	Percent of Total	Dollar Volume (in millions)	Percent of Total
Commercial Banks	2,417	12.8	5,966	12.9
Farmers Home Administration	1,285	6.8	3,212	6.9
Federal Land Bank	3,687	19.5	13,402	28.9
Life Insurance Companies	4,288	22.7	6,317	13.6
Individuals and Others	7,218	38.2	17,408	37.6
Totals	18,895	100.0	46,305	100.0

Source: *Monthly Review,* Federal Reserve Bank of Kansas City (November 1975), p. 13.

The increasing role played by the Federal Land Banks and their local associations in financing farm real estate needs has been accompanied by tighter reporting requirements initiated by the Federal Land Banks. The local associations have had to pay more attention in recent years to an accurate assessment of the financial condition of the loan applicant. This assessment is satisfied in part by a financial analysis (ratio analysis) of the farm business that is seeking the credit.

    Dudley's office is involved in making three major types of loans. First, loans are made to farmers both incorporated and unincorporated who are mainly involved in a farming-type operation. Second, loans are extended to individual economic units and business economic units that perform farm-related services. These loans involve the extension of credit to applicants who provide a custom-type service to the farmer. Third, loans are available to the owners of rural residences. Usually, the loans are limited to 85 percent of the value of the property offered as security for the credit. In almost every case the current market value of the property is used as the appraised value in setting the upper limit on the amount of the loan. The maturity period of the loans granted by the Farmers' Loan Associations range from 5 to 40 years.

    Last month Eliot Dudley had received from Howard Jackson a 12 month cash budget covering the current year for The Jackson Farm (TJF). Dudley had requested the budget as part of the information needed to evaluate Jackson's request for a loan to purchase 150 acres of prime farming land near Monterey (see The Jackson Farm, Part I). Dudley was impressed with the budget's detail and Jackson's overall understanding of the assumptions built into it. He had visited with Howard Jackson on two separate occasions at his farm to inspect the assets and get a feel for Jackson's grasp of the farming business. Dudley was well satisfied that even though Howard Jackson had retired from the steel manufacturing world, he was an energetic farmer with a thorough knowledge of his business. The land that Jackson desired to acquire would be utilized fully as part of the regular agribusiness operation that he owned and managed. The parcel recently had been appraised at $400 per acre for purposes of this loan request. Jackson also had assurances from the present owner that if he would pay the appraised price of the land, it would be sold to him. Dudley needed information from Jackson concerning the amount he actually wanted to borrow from the local association, as Jackson had indicated that a substantial amount of the purchase price would be met out of his own personal financial resources.

As usual, Dudley's secretary had arrived at the office before him and placed the morning mail along with another cup of coffee on his desk. On top of the stack was the hoped-for letter and set of documents from Howard Jackson.

Dudley quickly read the memorandum from Jackson (Exhibit 2). He then took the financial statements (Exhibits 3 and 4) and performed a preliminary analysis of the cash flow generating ability of the firm (Exhibit 6). He observed that during the past three years, the cash flow return on total assets had ranged from 5.53 percent to 10.01 percent. The past year was a bad one for most farms in the district served by the Verona Farmers' Loan Association. Dudley estimated that 80 percent of all farm businesses in the region would report a negative net farm income before tax. With a high degree of confidence, Dudley felt that TJF would continue to earn at least a cash flow return on total assets of 8 percent. This compared favorably to a norm for farms in the Verona district of 6.9 percent.

At this time Robert Walker, a credit officer who worked for Dudley, returned with the loan amortization schedule that he had been directed to draw up a few minutes earlier. Jackson's loan request of $25,500 would carry an annual interest rate of 9 percent and be paid off in equal annual installments over a 10-year period, as indicated in Exhibit 7.

Dudley now pulled three tabulations from his file cabinet (Exhibits 8, 9, and 10). With reference to Exhibit 8, Dudley noted that farms with outstanding debt in the Fifth District (which included Verona) were probably paying at least 7 percent on the loans. Exhibit 9 contains a common size balance sheet for the entire U.S. farming sector. Exhibit 10 contains a summary of data compiled over the years by Dudley. Dudley recognized many years ago the value of standards of comparison in the analysis of financial statements. He took it upon himself to review every year the financial characteristics of the farms that had been successful in obtaining credit at his office. With this information, Dudley continued with his evaluation of Howard Jackson's loan request.

EXHIBIT 2

January 8

Mr. Eliot Dudley, Manager
Farmers' Loan Association
Verona, VA 24482

Dear Mr. Dudley:

I enjoyed talking with you last week and appreciate the opportunity which I had to show you around The Jackson Farm. I hope I was able to give you a clear picture of our operation.

Enclosed you will find the three documents that you requested at our last meeting. The balance sheets (Exhibit 3), income statements (Exhibit 4), and loan amortization schedule (Exhibit 5) are attached. The latter schedule was prepared by my commercial bank. At my preference I pay the bank one-twelfth of the annual payment each month, even though the interest expense is computed on an annual basis.

Apart from my incorporated business, you also inquired as to the percentage of my adjusted gross (personal) income that income tax payments absorbed during the past three years. The average has been 25 percent. As most of my outside income from personal sources is from my pension and a securities portfolio designed for safety of income, I do not believe this 25 percent figure will change much over the next few years.

Finally, I plan to use $34,500 of savings to help purchase the subject 150-acre parcel. Thus, I am asking for a mortgage loan of $25,500, which I would like to pay off over a ten-year period.

If you need any further information related to this matter, please phone or write and I will attend to the request immediately.

Sincerely,

Howard Jackson
The Jackson Farm

HJ/jc
Enclosures

EXHIBIT 3

The Jackson Farm-II

Balance Sheets
December 31

	Most Recent Year	1 Year Ago	2 Years Ago
Cash	$ 6,800	$ 6,150	$ 4,969
Accounts Receivable	2,000	1,600	1,293
Feed and seed	5,000	4,000	3,232
Livestock held for sale	9,340	8,000	6,464
Total current assets	$ 23,140	$ 19,750	$ 15,958
Hereford cattle (held for breeding)	$ 11,000	$ 10,800	$ 8,725
Ewes (held for breeding)	3,150	3,100	2,428
Machinery and equipment	9,200	7,900	6,364
Autos and trucks	6,100	5,174	4,189
Total intermediate assets	$ 29,450	$ 26,974	$ 21,706
Real estate	$121,500	$121,500	$121,500
Homes and buildings	90,000	90,000	90,000
Total fixed assets	$211,500	$211,500	$211,500
Total assets	$264,090	$258,224	$249,164
Accounts payable	$ 7,000	$ 3,000	$ 5,000
Current portion of long-term debt	1,946	1,802	1,668
Total current liabilities	$ 8,946	$ 4,802	$ 6,668
Mortgage (held by local commercial bank)	$ 63,729	$ 65,675	$ 67,477
Common stock (family owned)	166,326	166,326	166,326
Retained earnings	25,089	21,421	8,693
Total liabilities and equity	$264,090	$258,224	$249,164

EXHIBIT 4

The Jackson Farm - II

Income Statements
December 31

	Most Recent Year	1 Year Ago	2 Years Ago
Net Sales	$55,000	$57,000	$54,000
Cost of goods sold	24,750	21,860	24,900
Gross profit	$30,250	$35,140	$29,100
Operating expenses	13,350[1]	7,190	6,800
Depreciation	4,500	4,000	3,700
Administrative expenses	2,300	2,100	1,800
Interest expense	5,398	5,532	5,655
Farm income before tax	$ 4,702	$16,318	$11,145
Tax (.22)	1,034	3,590	2,452
Net farm income	$ 3,668	$12,728	$ 8,693
Dividends paid	0	0	0
To retained earnings	$ 3,668	$12,728	$ 8,693

[1]Includes a $5,000 expenditure to replace roof and make structural improvements to the main barn.

EXHIBIT 5

The Jackson Farm - II

Repayment Schedule of Outstanding
8% Real Estate Loan

End of Year	Total Payment	Principal	Interest	Balance
0				$70,690
1	$7,200	$1,545	$5,655	$69,145
2	$7,200	$1,668	$5,532	$67,477
3	$7,200	$1,802	$5,398	$65,675
4	$7,200	$1,946	$5,254	$63,729
5	$7,200	$2,102	$5,098	$61,627
6	$7,200	$2,270	$4,930	$59,357
7	$7,200	$2,451	$4,749	$56,906
8	$7,200	$2,648	$4,552	$54,258
9	$7,200	$2,859	$4,341	$51,399
10	$7,200	$3,088	$4,112	$48,311
11	$7,200	$3,335	$3,865	$44,976
12	$7,200	$3,602	$3,598	$41,374
13	$7,200	$3,890	$3,310	$37,484
14	$7,200	$4,201	$2,999	$33,283
15	$7,200	$4,537	$2,663	$28,746
16	$7,200	$4,900	$2,300	$23,846
17	$7,200	$5,292	$1,908	$18,554
18	$7,200	$5,716	$1,484	$12,838
19	$7,200	$6,173	$1,027	$ 6,665
20	$7,200	$6,665	$ 535	$ 0

EXHIBIT 6

The Jackson Farm - II

Preliminary Analysis of Cash Flow Return

	Most Recent Year	1 Year Ago	2 Years Ago
Farm income before tax	$ 4,702	$ 16,318	$ 11,145
Depreciation expense	4,500	4,000	3,700
Interest expense	5,398	5,532	5,655
Before tax cash flow available to service financing costs	$ 14,600	$ 25,850	$ 20,500
Total investment in assets	$264,090	$258,224	$249,164
Before tax cash flow return on total assets	5.53%	10.01%	8.23%

EXHIBIT 7

The Jackson Farm - II

*Repayment Schedule for Requested 9% Real Estate
Loan with Farmers' Loan Association*

End of Year	Total Payment	Principal	Interest	Balance
0				$25,500
1	$3,973	$1,678	$2,295	$23,822
2	$3,973	$1,829	$2,144	$21,993
3	$3,973	$1,994	$1,979	$19,999
4	$3,973	$2,173	$1,800	$17,826
5	$3,973	$2,369	$1,604	$15,457
6	$3,973	$2,582	$1,391	$12,875
7	$3,973	$2,814	$1,159	$10,061
8	$3,973	$3,068	$ 905	$ 6,993
9	$3,973	$3,344	$ 629	$ 3,649
10	$3,973	$3,649	$ 324	$ 0

EXHIBIT 8

Measures of Farm Operator's Financial Position
Fifth Federal Reserve District, 1970

Item	Unit	Average Per Farm Reporting
Average size of farm	acres	172
Value of land and buildings per farm	dollars	58,761
Net cash farm income per farm	dollars	3,523
Off-farm income per farm	dollars	6,755
Total net cash income per farm	dollars	10,278
Total debt per farm	dollars	15,717

Source: *Economic Review,* Federal Reserve Bank of Richmond (May/June 1975), p. 15.

EXHIBIT 9

U.S. Farming Sector Percentage Balance Sheet
Average for 1970-1972

Assets		Liabilities and Equity	
Cash and deposits	3.9%	Real estate debt	9.3%
U.S. savings bonds	1.1	Other debt	10.0
Investment in		Equity	80.7
cooperatives	2.4		
Crops	3.5		
Livestock	7.7		
Machinery and vehicles	10.6		
Household equipment			
and furnishings	3.3		
Real estate	67.5		
Total	100.0%	Total	100.0%

Source: *Economic Report of the President,* Washington, U.S. Government Printing Office, 1974, p.349.

EXHIBIT 10

Verona Farm Credit District
Standard Financial Relationships[1]
(Based on Loans Granted)
Classification: Hereford Cattle

Ratio	Standard
Current ratio	2.42
Acid test ratio	1.00
Intermediate ratio[2]	5.67
Inventory turnover (regular) (COGS/EI)	1.68
Inventory turnover (including intermediate inventory of livestock)	.80
Debt ratio	24.0%
Debt-to-net-worth ratio	36.5%
Interest coverage ratio	3.00
Cash-flow coverage ratio	3.20
Gross profit margin	54.5%
Net profit margin	12.0%
Total asset turnover	0.29
Return on assets	3.5%
Return on common stock equity	not available

[1] These standard relationships were last updated twelve months ago. They represent the composite experience of three years.

[2] Current and intermediate assets divided by current and intermediate debt.

QUESTIONS AND PROBLEMS

1. Perform a preliminary financial ratio analysis based upon the three years of financial statements provided for The Jackson Farm. In this initial portion of your overall analysis, utilize the standard relationships computed by Dudley (Exhibit 10).

2. Expand your analysis to include consideration of information provided in Exhibits 6, 8, and 9 where useful. Draw upon any data in The Jackson Farm, Part I that might affect this loan request.

3. Comment upon possible security arrangements for this loan. What other information might prove useful to Dudley?

4. Should Dudley grant the loan requested by Jackson?

Case 7

CONNALLY OIL COMPANY, INC.

(Cash Budgeting and Pro Forma Statements)

The Connally Oil Company was founded in 1957 by J. Edward Connally. Connally's beginning in the oil industry came through a joint venture with several associates in drilling two oil wells in north central Texas. Although the drilling venture proved to be only moderately successful in terms of oil and gas reserves discovered, Connally took an active role in the decision-making process, which initiated a career in the oil and gas industry. During the ensuing years, he came to understand the necessary ingredients for discovering oil. This insight was complemented with an equally essential ability for attracting the necessary financing for the drilling projects. As he became better known within financial circles throughout the country, he was able to finance a drilling site by traveling to one of several major cities and visiting with acquaintances having sufficient income to justify their entrance into high-risk investments. Not only did the investment offer potential financial rewards, but the tax incentive for an individual in a relatively high tax bracket was also a major consideration. For these reasons, and as a result of Connally being able to gain the confidence of prospective investors, the company encountered significant growth in terms of its drilling programs.

The investment process utilized by Connally Oil is a "turnkey" arrangement whereby investors pay a fixed sum of money for their part of the drilling and an additional amount if the well is completed. Completion depends upon whether or not tests indicate that the substructure is such that production of the well would be profitable. In other words, the drilling process occurs in two phases. First, an investment is made to drill to a certain depth (drilling costs). After testing the structure, a decision is made whether or not to expend the funds required to finalize the production capability of the well (completion costs). For instance, in a given drilling venture, an investor having a 1/16th interest might pay $12,500 for drilling costs, and if a decision is made to complete the well, an additional $5,000 is required. This investment entitles the individual to 1/16th of the net income resulting from the extraction of the oil and/or gas. Furthermore, the investor receives tax benefits in the form of being permitted to expense the major portion of the investment in the present year; with the remaining part being capitalized and depreciated over the "expected" life of the project. Connally, in turn, is reponsible for the drilling and completion of the site. However, in addition to maintaining an interest in most wells, company profits result when the actual drilling costs are less than the turnkey fee being received. To illustrate, the owner of the land on which the drilling is to occur might receive 1/8 of all royalties. Of the remaining 7/8s, referred to as the "working interest," Connally may keep 1/8 of the well, selling the remaining 3/4ths of the investment to interested parties. In this instance, if the site is drilled and completed and if each "partner" pays $17,500 per 1/16th interest, Connally would receive $210,000, that is, $17,500 received from 12 investors (12/16ths). If the actual cost of drilling the well comes to $190,000, Connally would reap a $20,000 profit in the venture, as well as being entitled to 1/8th of all future net income from the investment. On the other hand, if the cost of drilling and completing is $240,000, a $30,000 loss would be incurred. Thus, Connally is in essence underwriting a portion of the risk by guaranteeing the investor a certain part of the oil reserves, if the venture is successful, at a specified price, regardless of the actual outlays for drilling and completing.

A second area of service provided by Connally Oil is the operation of the completed sites. In this regard, when a drilling venture is productive, the investors contract with Connally Oil for services performed in the day-to-day operation and maintenance of the well. For example, the working-interest owners would generally pay $50 to Connally Oil on a monthly basis for personnel employed in maintaining the well. Also, a record is kept of all expenses paid in operating the well, for which the participants are billed on a cost basis. The reimbursement for both the personnel salaries and expenses encountered are due within 30 days.

Although the business has proven to be quite profitable, Connally Oil, like many small business organizations, often fails to anticipate adequately its cash needs within the planning horizon of one year. As a new employee, you have been called upon to develop a monthly cash budget for the forthcoming year and a corresponding pro forma income statement and balance sheet. You have been provided the following information:

1. Recent financial statements (Exhibits 1 and 2).
2. The average cost of drilling and completing an exploratory site (Exhibit 3).
3. A summary of existing wells (Exhibit 4).
4. A projection of the drilling program for the coming 12 months (Exhibit 5).
5. The company dividend policy is to pay 20 percent of earnings after taxes, payable in January of the following year.
6. Capital expenditures for the forthcoming year should approximate $143,000, determined as follows:

Type of Expenditure	Month of Expenditure	Amount
Office Building and Equipment	February	$ 40,000.
Service Equipment	April	4,000.
Production Equipment	evenly throughout the year	27,000.
Leasehold Investments	1/2 in April 1/2 in August	72,000.
		$143,000.

Depreciation schedules for 1978 reflect the following amounts:

Service Equipment (maintenance of wells)	$ 5,480.
Production Equipment	52,100.
Office Building and Equipment (administrative)	29,460.

7. Recurring administrative expenses are normally paid in the month incurred; other payables within 30 days unless otherwise specified.

CASE REQUIREMENT

With the foregoing information, prepare the requested financial statements. Also specifically list your assumptions in the preparation of these statements. In developing the cash budget, the ending cash balance for each month should be ascertained. In making the computations, do not modify the existing marketable securities, the notes payable, except as called for in the case or the long-term debt. Only after your results are presented to management will these items be changed.

EXHIBIT 1

Connally Oil Company, Inc.

Balance Sheet, December 31, 1977

<u>Assets</u>

Current Assets:

Cash	$ 327,234
Marketable Securities	43,718
Accounts Receivable[1]	11,550
Inventory[2]	452,111
Office Supplies	5,414
Wells-in-Progress[3]	632,000
Total Current Assets	$1,472,027

Plant and Equipment (Net):

Office Building and Equipment	$ 460,376
Production Equipment	445,000
Service Equipment	18,522
Total Plant and Equipment	$ 923,898
Leasehold Investment	$ 400,000
Total Assets	$2,795,925

[1] Accounts receivable result from the extension of credit for services performed in maintenance of the production in behalf of the owners having a working interest in the wells. While receivables might be outstanding beyond the 30 days extension of credit, bad debts are negligible.

[2] Inventory consists of drilling materials, e.g., pipe, pump units, and other necessary drilling equipment. The level of inventory is closely related to the number of wells drilled in any given year. Furthermore, as inventory is drawn upon, it is charged out at cost against the particular well using the inventory.

[3] The wells in progress represent four wells, with two of the sites being at the end of the drilling process, but with no completion decision having yet been made, and the other two locations have been drilled and successfully completed, but simply have not been closed out in the financial statements.

EXHIBIT 1 (cont'd)

Connally Oil Company, Inc.

Balance Sheet, December 31, 1977

Liabilities and Net Worth

Current Liabilities:	
Dividend Payable[4]	$ 38,484
Accounts Payable[5]	320,422
Notes Payable[6]	20,000
Advanced Payments[7]	715,000
Interest Payable	833
Profit Sharing Plan[8]	39,727
Income Taxes Payable[9]	52,620
Total Current Liabilities	$1,187,086
Long-Term Liabilities[10]	$ 180,000
Total Liabilities	$1,367,086
Net Worth:	
Common Stock (par $10)	$ 100,000
Paid in Surplus	503,159
Retained Earnings	825,680
Total Net Worth	$1,428,839
Total Liabilities and Net Worth	$2,795,925

[4]Dividends are payable in January.

[5]Accounts payable are outstanding for 30 days and normally represent the accrual of drilling and completion expenses, costs incurred in the servicing of wells, and production expenses attributable to Connally Oil Company's working interest. However, at the 1977 balance sheet date, accounts payable relate only to drilling and completion costs.

[6]Notes payable will be due on July 31 with the interest payable for the preceding year (August 1, 1977 - July 31, 1978). Five months of interest expense has been accrued for 1977 at 10 percent.

[7]Advanced payments represent money received from investors, for which the well in question has not been completed. Typically 3/4ths of the prospective oil well is sold to investors, 1/8th royalty goes to the land owners, and 1/8th is received by Connally Oil Company. Also the payments are generally received during the month of drilling. The average fee for a 1/16th owner is $12,500 for drilling and $5,000 for completion.

[8]The profit-sharing plan stipulates that 10 percent of taxable income, before subtracting the profit sharing contribution for the year, is to be paid to a designated trust department by April 30 of the ensuing year.

[9]Income taxes payable are to come due on January 15 in the amount of $37,500, the last quarterly payment for 1977. The remaining $15,120 is to be paid April 15.

[10]Interest is payable quarterly beginning March 31, with the rate being 9 percent. The principal of this indebtedness should not change during 1978.

EXHIBIT 2

Connally Oil Company, Inc.

Income Statement
January 1 - December 31, 1977

Exploration:[1]

Sales		$4,690,000
Direct Cost of Drilling and Completing		4,350,700
Exploration Income	$	339,300
Service:[2]		
Service Fees	$	115,282
Expenses		
Operational Salaries		70,000
Maintenance and Repairs of Producing Wells		21,611
Travel Expense		8,212
Supplies		6,216
Depreciation		4,630
Total Expense	$	110,669
Service Income	$	4,613
Production Income:[3]		
Royalties	$	408,624
Operating Expenses		
Depreciation		44,200
Production Expenses		16,462
Depletion[4]		112,665
Total Operating Expenses	$	173,327
Net Production Income	$	235,297

[1] Sales represent the collection of funds for the investors' interest in the wells.

[2] The "service" segment of the income statement details the receipts and expenses related to the maintenance of the existing production as set forth in the contract with the investors. The expenses shown in this category are billed to the participants in relationship to their ownership interest in the wells. While the fees billed in 1977 exceed the expenses by $4,613, the difference between these receipts and expenses has historically been negligible. Also, experience indicates the expenses, with the exception of depreciation, to be variable relative to the number of wells being operated and occurring evenly throughout the year.

[3] Production income is the result of Connally Oil's working interest in the wells.

[4] Depletion for each well is calculated based upon the allowable percentage depletion or cost depletion, selecting the alternative yielding the higher figure. However, this amount has normally approximated 27 percent of gross receipts.

EXHIBIT 2 (cont'd)

Connally Oil Company, Inc.

Income Statement
January 1 - December 31, 1977

Administrative Expenses

Office Salary[5]	$	86,250
Field Salary[6]		36,125
Depreciation		28,414
Travel and Entertainment[5]		12,821
Profit-Sharing Contribution		39,727
Miscellaneous Expenses[5]		6,277
Total Administrative Expenses	$	207,614
Operating Profits	$	371,596
Interest Income from Marketable Securities[6]		3,279
Interest Expense		17,333
Earnings before Taxes	$	357.542
Taxes[7]		165,120
Earnings after Taxes	$	192,422

[5]These expenses vary directly with exploration sales.

[6]The income from these securities is received quarterly at a 7.5 percent annual rate.

[7]Taxes are based upon 22 percent for $25,000 and 48 percent for any amount exceeding the $25,000, (disregard investment tax credit).

EXHIBIT 3

Connally Oil Company, Inc.

Average Cost of Drilling
and Completion

Cost of Drilling	
Drilling Rig Operation	$100,000
Pipe	18,000
Other Equipment	5,250
Supplies	9,350
Total Drilling Costs	$132,600
Cost of Completion	
Pipe	$ 26,000
Other Equipment	11,700
Supplies	24,200
Total Completion Cost	$ 61,900
Total Cost of Drilling and Completion	$194,500

EXHIBIT 4

Connally Oil Company, Inc.

Existing Production
December 31, 1977

Number of Wells Remaining	Age of Site(Years)[1]	Number of Wells Drilled	Number of Wells Completed[4]	Percentage of Oil Revenues
18	0 - .99	24[2]	18[3]	16.9
32	1 - 2.99	40	32	27.0
45	3 - 5.99	66	50	30.1
28	6 - 9.99	45	34	18.2
19	10 - 14.99	35	28	6.4
6	15 - over	36	24	1.4
148		246	186	100.0

[1]The average life of production property for Connally Oil Company has been 15 years. Also the number of wells within an age category is evenly divided between years, e.g., in classification 1 - 2.99 years, the 32 wells are almost equally divided between 1 - 1.99 and 2.99 years.

[2]Includes the four wells in process.

[3]Excludes the two wells in process, for which a completion decision has yet to be made.

[4]The relatively high rate of completion is due to the restriction of Connally Oil to proven oil fields.

EXHIBIT 5

Connally Oil Company, Inc.

1978 Drilling Program

Month	Number of Sites to be Started[1]
January	2
February	3
March	4
April	1
May	2
June	2
July	2
August	3
September	3
October	4
November	2
December	1
Total	29

[1] The drilling and completion of a well normally requires approximately 30 days. Another 30-day lag exists between the oil production and the receipt of money from the pipeline company from the sale of the oil. For example, the receipt for oil production in January comes at the end of February.

Section 2

Working
Capital
Management

Case 1

M&M NOVELTIES, INC.
(Working Capital Management—Overview)

In the fall of 1973, Harry Marchant and Peter Mitchell formed M & M Novelties, Inc. Both men had worked previously for the Marz Toy Company, where Marchant was a new products engineer and Mitchell was a regional sales manager. They had discussed the idea of forming their own company for some time, and the idea finally came into being with the production of a new game that Marchant invented called "Big Money." Both men were convinced of the potential for the game and felt that it would be the ideal vehicle to get their firm off the ground.

The firm was incorporated in October 1973 and began operations with a total of $150,000 in capital. A group of 10 investors put up $96,000 in equity capital, with the remainder of the funds coming from a $30,000 loan from a life insurance company and a line of credit from the firm's bank.

During the first year, sales were even better than anticipated, and the "good times" seemed to continue throughout most of the firm's second year. In fact, during the last quarter the firm had acquired $12,500 worth of fixed assets, which were to be used to expand the productive capacity for both existing and planned product lines. From both a production efficiency and sales point of view, the firm's owners were very pleased with the company's performance in its short two-year history. However, the firm has been plagued with cash flow problems. In the past, the financing decisions of the firm had been more evolutionary than planned, resulting in the demise of the firm's working capital to a point that seriously jeopardized its ability to obtain additional credit. The sad state of the firm's financial affairs was highlighted by its inability to get the bank to raise the limit on its line of credit for the coming year. The bank cited the firm's continued increase in the use of debt financing and deteriorating working capital position as the basis for its decision.

In light of this latest financial crisis, the firm's board of directors (Marchant served as chairman, Mitchell as company president) decided to hire a controller to take over the duties of chief financial officer in charge of accounting and finance. In the past, the firm had simply relied on the services of an external CPA firm to handle its accounting and payroll needs with no one being assigned responsibility for the management of the internal financial affairs of the company.

After a brief search, Barry Whitehead was hired to take over the duties of the newly created position of Vice-President for Accounting and Finance. Barry had his CPA and also had prior work experience in banking as a commercial lending officer. The first assignment for Whitehead was to prescribe a cure for the firm's immediate working capital deficiencies and to set forth a financing plan or strategy that would prevent the recurring cash flow problems experienced over the past two years.

QUESTIONS

1. The company's most recent balance sheet and income statement are contained in Exhibit 1:

EXHIBIT 1

M & M Novelties, Inc.

Balance Sheet
12/31/75
(Thousands)

Cash	$ 5.0	Accounts Payable &	$ 22.5
Accounts Receivable	45.0	Accrued Expenses	
		Notes Payable[1]	37.5
Inventory	40.0	Current Liabilities	60.0
Current Assets	90.0	Long-Term Debt[2]	30.0
Net Plant & Equipment	100.0	Common Stock ($1 par)	20.0
		Paid-In Capital	76.0
		Retained Earnings	4.0
	$190.0		$190.0

[1]Made up of a $10,000 note from the First Bank and Trust of Westing, Ohio, carrying a 10 percent rate of interest, and the remainder coming from a $40,000 line of credit. The line of credit agreement calls for an annual interest rate of 14 percent and a 1/4 of one percent fee on the unused portion.

[2]The long-term debt was obtained from the Mutual of Syracuse Life Insurance Company and is due in full in 1986, carrying a 13.80 percent rate of interest.

EXHIBIT 1 (cont'd)

M & M Novelties, Inc.

Income Statement
For the Year Ended
12/31/75
(Thousands)

Sales (Net)	$200
Cost of Goods Sold	(85)
Gross Profit	115
Operating Expenses	
Wages and Salaries	(60)
Rent	(10)
Utilities	(8)
	(78)
Depreciation	(10)
Net Operating Income	27
Interest Expense	(9)
Earnings Before Taxes	18
Federal Taxes	(4)
Net Profit	$14

1a. Compute the firm's current ratio, debt ratio (total liabilities/total assets), and times interest earned ratio using the data in Exhibit 1.

1b. Approximate norms for the toy industry appropriate to the size of M & M are as follows:

Ratio	Norm[1]
Current Ratio	1.70 - 2.50
Debt Ratio	40% - 50%
Times Interest Earned	4.00 - 5.50

[1]You may assume that the norms have not varied significantly over the past two years.

Do you agree with the bank's decision to refuse the firm's request to increase its line of credit? Discuss briefly.

1c. Prepare a statement of sources and uses of working capital for the quarter ended 12/31/75 if the net income for the quarter was $4,000 and depreciation expense was $2,500. Use the information contained in Exhibit 2 to complete your answer. Also, the firm paid quarterly dividends to common totaling $2,000.

1d. What does the source and use statement prepared in 1c tell you about the firm's most recent contribution to its working capital problem (i.e., discuss the firm's principal sources and uses of funds and how they have impaired the firm's working capital position).

1e. What do you think should be Whitehead's recommendation for solving the firm's immediate working capital deficiency? Explain the course of action you would recommend as well as any alternatives that might be available. (Do not devise a specific plan; address yourself to the alternative sources of financing open to M & M that would improve the firm's financial condition.)

2. The balance sheets for the past eight quarters are presented in Exhibit 2.

EXHIBIT 2

(Thousands)

	Net Fixed Assets	Current Assets	Total Assets	A/P & Acc. Exp.	Notes Payable	Long-Term Debt	Common Equity	To Liab and
3/31/74	86	88	174	22.0	26.0	30	96	1
6/30/74	86	92	178	23.0	29.0	30	96	1
9/30/74	86	94	180	23.5	29.5	30	97	1
12/31/74	88	89	177	22.5	27.5	30	97	1
3/31/75	89	92	181	23.0	31.0	30	97	1
6/30/75	89	94	183	23.5	31.5	30	98	1
9/30/75	90	96	186	24.0	34.0	30	98	1
12/31/75	100	90	190	22.5	37.5	30	100	1

2a. Based on the information in Exhibit 2, compute the firm's current ratio and debt ratio for each of the past eight quarters.

2b. Describe verbally the "method followed by M & M in financing the firm's assets (i.e., when new financing was needed, how was it obtained?). Note the relationship between current assets and accounts payable.

3. Exhibit 3 contains the firm's estimates of its needs for assets (funds) over the next eight quarters, along with its estimated net income and dividends to common stock.

EXHIBIT 3

(Thousands)

Quarter Ending	Net Plant and Equipment	Net Income[1]	Common Dividends/Share[2]	Current Assets
3/31/76	100	3.0	.05	92
6/30/76	100	3.0	.05	96
9/30/76	100	4.0	.05	98
12/31/76	100	4.0	.05	92
3/31/77	101	3.0	.10	94
6/30/77	101	3.0	.10	98
9/30/77	108	4.0	.10	100
12/31/77	110	4.0	.10	94

[1]These estimates are purposely "conservative."

[2]In dollars, the firm plans to cut its cash dividend to $.05 per share for the coming year to provide needed equity capital.

3a. Devise a plan that will solve the firm's immediate working capital problem by 3/31/76 (based on your recommendations in 1e).

3b. Based upon your answer to 3a and given the information provided in Exhibit 3, prepare a set of pro forma balance sheets similar to the historical statements in Exhibit 2. In your financing plan make sure that permanent asset requirements are financed with permanent sources of funds and temporary asset needs are financed with temporary sources of funds.

3c. Compute current ratios and debt ratios for the pro forma statements prepared in 3b.

3d. Discuss the "flexibility" of your financing plan with respect to the ease of adjusting to drops in income below projected levels; i.e., how subject is the firm to liquidity crises under your proposed financing plan for "hedging" the financing of permanent and temporary assets?

Case 2

G. W. BARNES MFG. COMPANY

(Investing in Accounts Receivable)

Barnes' principal products are dyed and treated nylon yarns for carpets, and dyed, treated polyester film for decorative and other applications. The company has recently introduced several new products: the Barnes Antistatic yarn finish, dyed polyester yarns for carpets, and dyed yarns for the drapery and upholstery fields. During the last 10 years the firm has grown very rapidly from a closely held, family corporation with total assets of less than $5,000,000 to one of the top three firms in the industry with assets totaling over $25,000,000. During that period Barnes increased its use of long-term debt considerably, from little more than $400,000 in 1965 to over $8,000,000 in 1974. This rather rapid growth in assets and the use of financial leverage have led the company's new president, Henley Barnes, Jr., to the conclusion that the firm's investment and financing policies should be carefully reviewed before embarking on any new investments.

The new president took over in June 1974 as a result of the failing health of his father, who had guided the firm through its rapid expansion in the 1960s. The senior Barnes suffered a heart attack in the fall of 1973 and was forced to retire from the active day-to-day operations of the company. He retained the chairmanship of the board of directors and was available to provide guidance during the important transition period. The younger Barnes has been with the company for the past five years following graduation from college and a short period of employment with a major New York bank. During his five-year tenure, Barnes made a point of trying to serve in as many of the functional areas of the firm as possible to develop a complete understanding of its operation. Among the firm's employees the new president gained the reputation for being "intolerant" of waste and inefficiency. In fact, Barnes has been known to dismiss long-time employees on the spot for what he considered gross errors in judgment.

In the nine months since the change in leadership, a number of changes have been instituted in both the firm's capital investment review procedures and financing policies. Little attention, however, has been given to the working capital decisions, with the exception of cash management, which has been reviewed very carefully, and new budgetary procedures implemented. Specifically, no attempt as yet has been made to review the firm's policies with regard to the extension of credit and the resulting investment in accounts receivable. Benjamin Buckner, who serves as controller, suggested that the firm might consider its present credit terms in light of the effects of either raising or lowering the cash discount on overall sales, profits, and investment in receivables. Following his suggestion, Barnes asked that the controller proceed with his proposed analysis of the firm's credit policies and report to him any suggestion for change.

Buckner, in turn, assigned the project to his assistant, who is the firm's financial analyst. The assistant was asked to prepare a report encompassing the following set of alternative credit policies:

EXHIBIT 1

Credit Policy	Estimated Sales[1]	Credit Terms
A	$34,000,000	4/10, net 45
B	32,000,000	3/10, net 45
C	30,000,000	2/10, net 45
D	28,000,000	1/10, net 45

[1]The sales estimates were prepared by the sales manager and represent what he believes are very pessimistic estimates of what might result from suggested changes in the firm's credit terms.

After he had collected the sales data for each of the proposed credit policies, the analyst sought out information concerning the proportion of the firm's existing credit sales taking advantage of the cash discount. Further, realizing that a change in the cash discount would probably lead to a change in both the proportion of the customers taking the discount and the resulting average collection period, the analyst enlisted the aid of the firm's credit department to generate the following projections:

EXHIBIT 2

Credit Policy	Customers Taking Discount (%)[1]	Average Collection Period[1]
A	80	28 days
B	60	29 days
C[2]	30	30 days
D	10	40 days

[1]Once again, these estimates represent "pessimistic" projections since the analyst wants to build an element of conservatism into his final choice of credit terms.

[2]Credit policy C is the firm's present policy.

In an effort to determine marginal profits on new sales, the analyst has estimated variable cash operating expenses for the existing plant facility at approximately 76.5 percent of sales. Also, given that the company is presently operating at 75 percent capacity, he estimates that average total cost is roughly 90 percent of sales. Based on these estimates, the analyst prepared the following report and recommendation for Buckner:

EXHIBIT 3

	Credit Policy			
	A	B	C	D
Sales	$34,000,000	32,000,000	30,000,000	28,000,000
Cash Discounts[1]	(1,088,000)	(576,000)	(180,000)	(28,000)
Operating Expenses	(30,600,000)	(28,800,000)	(27,000,000)	(25,200,000)
Net Operating Income	$ 2,312,000	2,624,000	2,820,000	2,772,000
Accounts Receivable[2]	$ 2,644,444	2,577,778	2,500,000	.3,111,111
Return on Investment[3]	87.4%	101.8%	112.8%	89.1%

[1]Cash discounts equal credit sales times proportion of sales on which the discount is taken times the discount percentage.

[2]The level of accounts receivable was computed using the expected average collection period and projected credit sales. For example, the level of accounts receivable for credit policy A was estimated using the relation:

$$\text{Average Collection Period} = 28 \text{ days} = \frac{\text{Accounts Receivable}}{\text{Credit Sales}/360}$$

[3]Return on investment in accounts receivable was found by dividing net operating income by the level of investment in accounts receivable.

Based on the results presented in Exhibit 3, the financial analyst recommended that the firm continue its present policy of offering a 2 percent cash discount for payment within 10 days, with the net amount due in 45 days. After receiving the report, Buckner suggested that they get together to discuss the proposal when he had had time to review it thoroughly.

QUESTIONS

1. Based on the information given in the case, do you agree with the analyst's solution and accompanying recommendation? Discuss. Based on a 30 percent before tax, required return on investment in new accounts receivable, prepare a work sheet to support your policy recommendation.

2. If by altering credit terms the firm's bad debt losses had been increased from 2 percent of credit sales (assume that these losses were not included in the case analysis) under the present policy (C) to 3 percent of all credit sales for policy D and decreased to 1.5 percent for policy A and 1.75 percent for policy B, would this have affected your analysis? Prepare an appropriate work sheet to support your answer.

Case 3

McCLURKINS BEVERAGE, INC.

(Inventory Management)

McClurkins Beverage, Inc. is a soft drink distributor serving the northeastern United States, having done so for the past 20 years. Started by John McClurkin, the firm has prospered during this time-span, but a recessionary period that began 12 months ago has resulted in a moderate reduction in sales. As indicated in Exhibit 1, the company has encountered a substantial increase in sales volume during the most recent five years, with the only downturn occurring in the last year.

McClurkin has been quite proud of the company's growth pattern. However, he has also become aware of numerous difficulties resulting from the rapid growth, and is particularly disenchanted with his ability to maintain adequate control of the firm's operations. The need for change has been so extensive that McClurkin has been unable to continue a personal involvement in all decisions. One such specific area of concern has been in inventory management. With the growth in revenues, a concurrent increase in inventories has been observed, and McClurkin questions the advisability of the large surge in inventory stocks. James Menielle, the production manager, takes great pride in not being out of stock when orders are received. Yet, McClurkin feels strongly that the base inventory is excessive, although he has no way of supporting his intuitive judgment. In addition, McClurkin wants a quantitative method of analysis, which could be used in determining the best inventory level for future planning periods. With such a technique, he states that he could relegate the decision-making process to the quantitative analysis; therefore, not having to be faced with a decision regarding inventory management.

In an effort to investigate any feasible methods for examining the company's inventory policies, McClurkin has visited the president of Management Consultants, Inc., for whom you are employed. The president has, in turn, assigned the effort to you, the express purpose being to develop an appropriate inventory model for McClurkins Beverage, Inc.

EXHIBIT 1

McClurkins Beverage, Inc.

Financial Data[1]

	1972	1973	1974	1975	1976
Sales	$987,000	$1,210,000	$1,460,000	$1,790,000	$1,705,000
Earnings before Interest and Taxes	59,220	95,071	172,545	173,550	164,280
Inventory[2]	393,000	484,000	768,421	895,000	920,700
Current Assets	393,000	714,400	1,012,000	1,275,700	1,310,000
Total Assets	493,500	864,285	1,327,272	1,704,762	1,794,737

[1]The asset items are year-end figures.

[2]The makeup of the inventory is 60% finished goods and 40% raw material and work-in-progress.

In visiting the corporate site, you have examined the corporation's records and interviewed the appropriate personnel, with the following discoveries:

1. The firm's sales tend to be moderately cyclical between quarters, with 70 percent of sales being distributed evenly throughout the second and third quarters. Furthermore, the remaining two quarters generally prove approximately equivalent in revenues. The marketing department projects the 1977 sales to be $1,860,000.

2. McClurkin's products are comprised of three lines, but the "College Delight" accounts for 85 percent of the total sales, and, in turn, a like percentage of inventory. The remaining two product lines are relatively new and represent no real problem in terms of inventory management.

3. The drinks are sold only to retail outlets (no vending machine sales) in a package containing 6 no-refund containers. The selling price is 75 cents.

4. In reviewing the cost of producing and packaging the 6-drink assembly, the following makeup is observed:

Material	$.30
Labor	.18
Container	.06
Allocation of overhead	.03

5. In the production process, management has experimented with several production plans, for example, producing in accordance with the sales level for the respective quarter. However, after such investigations, the corporate personnel consider the best production schedule to be one in which the production level remains constant throughout the year.

6. The production process involves three separate stages: (1) production of drink content, (2) manufacturing the containers, and (3) filling, sealing, and packaging the containers. Each procedure requires a machinery setup involving 7 hours, 5 hours, and 6 hours, respectively. The labor rate for the individuals performing the setups is $4.75, regardless of the process. In addition to the labor involved, several materials are essential in initializing the manufacturing stage. After careful inquiry, the cost by process is determined to be as follows:

Mixture setup	$48.
Container setup	17.
Packaging setup	24.

7. The 1976 inventory balance as noted in Exhibit 1 represents the current inventory position. As seen, the majority of the inventory (60 percent) is in the "finished goods" category, which, in fact, is the area of concern on the part of McClurkin.

8. Although the finished goods of the College Delight drink are considered excessive, no criterion has been developed for justifying a given base level. In talking with the responsible personnel, one of two preferences exist. First, as a result of pressure from the bank to improve the organization's profitability, McClurkin has been requested to be more aware of efficient asset utilization. Although no plan has been instigated, the financial officer has done some investigation into the financial position of similar businesses. For instance, the average inventory turnover of like firms, as recorded in the I. R. S. *Industrial Financial Ratios* is 4.63.[1] Typically the inventory is comprised of 55 percent finished goods inventory, the remainder being work-in-process and raw materials. As a second approach to the base inventory question, McClurkin, as opposed to Menielle's persistence to never have a stock out, indicates that a 10 percent probability of being out of finished goods inventory should be defined as acceptable. In reviewing the past variation in finished goods of College Delight over time, a standard deviation of $146,725 has been experienced.

[1]The inventory turnover ratio is expressed in terms of sales and the ending inventory balance.

Regardless of which criterion is to be applied, an immediate adjustment would simply not be feasible, but rather the modification in inventory would be a target to be achieved by year end.

9. Other costs relating to inventory management include: (a) monthly insurance premiums per $1,000 equaling $1.83, with the inventory being insured at 80 percent of cost of production; (b) storage facilities rented at a monthly cost of 10 cents per square yard, with each yard providing space for 90 containers; (c) depreciation of equipment relating to inventory maintenance at a fixed sum of $1,400; and (d) personnel costs of $45,467 in 1976 varying directly with the average amount of inventory.

10. The firm's opportunity cost for funds is 8 percent.

QUESTIONS

1. Most economic-order-quantity (EOQ) models are presented in terms of the optimal order quantity for *raw materials,* while the present case is addressing the issue of the optimal *production* level. What are the similarities and differences of the two applications?

2. Based upon either the target inventory turnover standard (4.63X) or the acceptable probability of being out of stock (10 percent), determine the appropriate year-end finished goods inventory level for the College Delight drink.

3. In light of the year-end target inventory for College Delight, how many units should be produced within the forthcoming planning horizon of one year?

4. Calculate the "economic order quantity" for the production level of College Delight drinks.

5. How many times would production be scheduled during the year?

6. What would be the approximate inventory level for College Delight at the conclusion of each quarter? Do these figures offer any indication as to a potential problem area by having a year-end target as opposed to possibly a quarterly inventory goal?

7. As best can be determined from the data given in the case, compute the average unit and dollar inventory for 1976 College Delight finished goods inventory. Also, from your calculations of the quarterly inventory balances in question 6, compute an expected average inventory level (units and dollars) for 1977. With the foregoing data, and knowing that production was scheduled 8 times during 1976, determine the annual benefits accruing to the firm as a result of adopting the proposed EOQ model?

8. Will the model do as McClurkin believes - eliminate the necessity of human judgment in the final decision?

Case 4

CALIFORNIA TRANSISTOR

(Cash Management)

Michael Broski is the assistant treasurer for California Transistor (Cal-Trans). He has been with the firm for nine years. The first six were spent within the technology ranks of the company as an electronics engineer. Broski, in fact, took his bachelor's degree in electronics engineering from a famous California-located university noted for its excellent faculty in all phases of engineering. After two years as a senior engineer for the organization, Broski indicated an interest in the administrative management of the firm. He spent one year as an analyst in the treasury department and has just completed his second as the assistant treasurer. During the latter three years, he has steeped himself in literature that focuses on the finance function of the corporate enterprise. In addition, he attended short courses and seminars by national management and accounting associations that dealt with most phases of the financial conduct of the firm. Within CalTrans, other cost accountants, cost analysts, financial analysts, and treasury analysts viewed Broski's rapid grasp of finance concepts as nothing short of phenomenal.

CalTrans is located on the outskirts of San Diego, California. The firm began in the middle 1950s as a small manufacturer of radio and television components. By the late 1950s, they had expanded into the actual installation and service of complete communications systems on navigable vessels. Ships from the U.S. Navy and from the tuna industry use the San Diego port facilities as a major repair yard. During the early years of the firm's activity, defense contracts typically accounted for 80 to 90 percent of annual revenues. Cal-Trans' management felt, however, that excessive reliance on defense contracts could lead to some very lean years with regard to business receipts. The company expanded during the 1960s into several related fields. Today CalTrans is active in the home entertainment market as well as the defense market. Transistors and integrated circuits are produced for a wide range of final products including radios, televisions, pocket calculators, citizens band receivers, stereo equipment, and ship communications systems. Defense-related business now accounts for 25 to 30 percent of the company's annual sales. This transition to a more diversified enterprise has tended to reduce the inherent "lumpiness" of cash receipts that plagues many small firms relying on defense contracts. In the early years of CalTrans' existence, progress payments on major contracts would often be months apart as the jobs moved toward completion. Currently, the firm enjoys a reasonably stable sales pattern over its fiscal year.

Broski has been studying the behavior of the company's daily and monthly net cash balances. Over the most recent 24 months, he observed that CalTrans' ending cash balance (by month) ranged between $144,000 and $205,000. Only twice during the period that he investigated had the daily closing cash balance even been as low as $100,000. Broski also noted that the firm had no outstanding short-term borrowings throughout these two years. This lead him to believe that CalTrans was carrying excessive cash balances; this was probably a tendency that had its roots in the period when defense contracts were the key revenue item for the company. This "first pass" analysis gained the attention of Donald Crawford, who is Broski's boss and CalTrans' treasurer. Crawford is 65 years old and due to retire on July 1 of this year. He has been CalTrans' only treasurer. Broski would like to move into Crawford's job upon his retirement and feels that the treasurer's recommendation might sew it up for him. He also knows that statements relating to excess cash balances being carried by the company will have to be made very tactfully and with Crawford's agreement. That bit of financial policymaking has always rested with the company treasurer. Broski decided that the best plan would be to present Crawford with a solid analysis of the problem and convince him that a reduction in balances held for transactions purposes would be in the best interests of the firm. As all key officers own considerable stock options, potential increases in corporate profitability usually are well received by management.

Earlier this year Broski attended a cash management seminar in Los Angeles, sponsored by the commercial bank with which CalTrans holds most of its deposits. The instructor spoke of the firm's cash balance as being "just another inventory." It was offered that the same principles that applied to the determination of an optimal stock of some raw material item also might be applied to the selection of an optimal average amount of transaction cash. Broski really liked that presentation. He walked away from it feeling that he could put it to work. He decided to adapt the basic economic order quantity model to his cash balance problem.

To make the model "workable," it is necessary to build an estimate of the fixed costs associated with adding to or subtracting from the company's inventory of cash. As CalTrans experienced no short-term borrowings within the past two years, Broski considered this element of the problem to be the fixed costs of liquidating a portion of the firm's portfolio of marketable securities.

In Exhibit 1, Broski has summarized the essential activities that occur whenever a liquidation of a part of the securities' portfolio takes place. In all of the firm's cost analysis procedures, it is assumed that a year consists of 264 working days. An eight-hour working day is also utilized in making wage and salary cost projections. Also, minutes of labor are converted into thousandths of an hour. The assistant treasurer felt that from the information in Exhibit 1,

EXHIBIT 1

California Transistor

Fixed Costs Associated With Securities Liquidation

Activity	Details
1. Long-distance phone calls.	Cost: $2.75
2. Assistant treasurer's time: 22 minutes	Annual salary for this position is $27,000
3. Typing of authorization letter, with three carbon copies, and careful proofreading: 17 minutes.	Annual salary for this position is $8,000
4. Carrying original authorization letter to treasurer, who reads and signs it; 2 minutes by same secretary as above, and 2 minutes by the treasurer.	Annual salary for the treasurer is $38,000
5. Movement of authorization letter just signed by the treasurer to the controller's office, followed by the opening of a new account, recording of the transaction, and proofing of the transaction; 2 minutes by same secretary as above, 10 minutes for account opening by general accountant, and 8 minutes for recording and proofing by the same general accountant.	Annual salary for the general accountant is $12,000
6. Fringe benefits incurred on above times.	Cost: $4.42
7. Brokerage fee on each transaction.	Cost: $7.74

he could make a decent estimate of the fixed cost of a security transaction (addition to the firm's cash account). CalTrans' marketable securities portfolio is usually concentrated in three major money market instruments: (1) treasury bills, (2) bankers' acceptances, and (3) prime commercial paper. A young analyst who works directly for Michael Broski supplied him with some recent rates of return on these types of securities (Exhibit 2). Broski expressed his concern to the analyst about the possibilities of high rates, such as those experienced during 1973 and 1974, continuing. His intuition or feel for the market led him to believe that short-term interest rates would be closer to 1975 levels during this next year than any other levels identified in Exhibit 2. Thus, Broski decided to use a 6 percent annual yield in this study as a reasonable return to expect from his firm's marketable securities portfolio. Then a review of cash flow patterns over the last five years, including the detailed examination of the most recent 24 months, led to a projection of a typical monthly cash outflow (or demand for cash for transactions purposes) of $800,000.

EXHIBIT 2

California Transistor

Selected Money Market Rates
(Annual Yields)

Year	Prime Commercial Paper: 90-119 Days	Bankers' Acceptances 90 Days	3-Month Treasury Bills
1972	4.66%	4.47%	4.07%
1973	8.20	8.08	7.04
1974	10.05	9.92	7.89
1975	6.26	6.30	5.84
Simple Average	7.29	7.19	6.21

Source: *Federal Reserve Bulletin,* Board of Governors of the Federal Reserve System (January 1976), p. A 27.

QUESTIONS

1. Determine the optimal cash withdrawal size from the CalTrans marketable securities portfolio during a typical month.

2. What is the total cost (in dollars) for the use of cash held for transactions purposes during the period of analysis?

3. What will be the firm's average cash balance during a typical month?

4. Assuming that fractional cash withdrawals or orders can be made, how often will an order be placed? The firm operates continually for 30 days each month.

5. If the company's cash balance at the start of a given month is $800,000, how much of that amount would initially be invested in securities?

6. Graph the behavior pattern of the $800,000 balance (mentioned above) over a 30-day month. In constructing your graph, round off the frequency of orders to the nearest whole day, and disregard separation of the balance between cash and securities.

7. To understand the logic of the model further, provide a graph that identifies in general: (1) the total cost function of holding the cash, (2) the fixed costs associated with cash transfers, and (3) the opportunity cost of earnings foregone by holding cash balances. Use dollar amounts to label the key points on the axes as they were previously computed in questions 1 and 2. Also, identify the major assumptions of this model in a cash management setting.

Section 3

Capital
Investment
Decisions

Case 1

DAVIDSON TRACTOR AND IMPLEMENT

(Capital Budgeting: Introductory)

Jack Murray felt especially good as he strolled toward the mahogany-paneled meeting room of the Davidson Tractor and Implement Company (DTI). That room was the focal point of the fourth floor of the DTI central administrative office building located in Des Moines, Iowa. Every Monday at 9:00 a.m. the key officers of the firm held what was referred to as "the management meeting." During this meeting the major decisions and policies that would have far-reaching effects on the company's future direction were made and formulated. Major capital expenditure proposals were either approved, rejected, or returned to the originating financial analyst for further development at the "horrible Monday" sessions, as they were sarcastically, and often accurately, referred to by those who made formal presentations before the top level management group. Murray had witnessed several employees, who were part of DTI's financial management training program, leave the firm because they were unable to stand the strain of the penetrating questions and comments typically posed by the management group at the weekly sessions. Murray however, thrived upon such intense personal contact and looked forward to each subsequent presentation. With those recurring sessions he improved his technique to present orally well-researched financial data.

The main reason that Murray had selected DTI as his initial place of employment upon completion of his undergraduate business degree from a major midwestern university was the firm's well-structured financial management training program. It consisted of two years of rotating job assignments wherein a basically talented individual could actually receive the equivalent of six to eight years of normal work experience. The training directors of DTI were fond of noting the difference between six year's experience one time, as opposed to one year's experience six times. The financial management training program, of course, was designed to produce the former. It was composed of six bench mark assignments including the areas of (1) payroll accounting, (2) data processing, (3) general accounting, (4) cost accounting, (5) cost analysis, and (6) financial analysis. The participant in the program filled an actual vacancy in the area for a specific period of time; this prevented "do nothing" assignments. When the area supervisor felt that the college graduate had made sufficient progress, it was recommended to the training director that the individual be transferred to the next higher assignment in the program. A more specific identification of program content is found in Exhibit 1. Rarely was the sequence of job assignments violated. This was because the work in the financial analysis department of the firm was considered the most important, and to operate effectively in that area meant a thorough knowledge of the company's financial control system. This was achieved through completion of the previous five assignments.

Murray had performed in an outstanding manner during his training program and was to be assigned to a final tractor assembly plant about 20 miles east of Windsor, Ontario, Canada, within a month. At the Branton Assembly Plant, he would be financial analysis supervisor, a responsible position for a man just about to turn 26 years of age. The vast majority of those who did complete the rigorous two-year internship within the financial organization of DTI did not automatically move into supervisory positions, but usually became floor leaders where the analysis work of about six to eight individuals was coordinated through a single, senior analyst.

Today, Murray would make a presentation to the management group of DTI dealing with mutually exclusive capital expenditure possibilities. DTI owns and operates the Cuyahoga Falls Transmission and Axle Plant, located a few miles north of Akron, Ohio. This full-scale production facility manufactures more than 50 percent of the transmissions and axles used in the complete line of tractors and harvesting equipment offered by DTI to the agribusiness industry. Due to the extensive machining processes performed on the steel parts that become part of the final transmission and axle assembly, a very large amount of steel shavings and other more bulky steel scrap is generated at this location. The steel scrap is sold as a by-product of the manufacturing operation to various firms involved in the recycling process from which comes several grades and types of usable steel. The scrap is classified as either rough or fine. The essential difference is that the fine scrap brings a considerably higher price in the marketplace than does the rough material. Both the rough and fine steel scrap are prepared for sale through a grinding and compressing procedure done by large machines called chip crushers. The selling prices and operating costs of the chip crushers, however, differ with regard to whether rough or fine scrap is being processed.

EXHIBIT 1

Davidson Tractor and Implement

Financial Training Program

Assignment and Description	Duration
1. Payroll Accounting: preparation, issue and validation of weekly and biweekly hourly and salary checks; perform overtime analysis by department and plant; prepare fringe-benefit cost analysis by department and plant.	3 months
2. Data Processing: learn to operate all equipment; run jobs and deliver reports on a timely basis; write a few, minor programs designed in conjunction with the cost accounting section.	4 months
3. General Accounting: learn all procedures relating to accounts receivable and payable, including authorization procedure that controls the printing of checks on the computer facility; prepare aging of accounts receivable report; participate in most phases of corporate cash management including the investment of excess cash and determination of minimum balance requirements at the firm's several deposit accounts.	4 months
4. Cost Accounting: participate in the annual setting of cost standards on all parts and assemblies used in the firm's manufacturing process; maintain data processing master file on all cost changes resulting in variances from the established standard; prepare the gross profit report by product line.	4 months
5. Cost Analysis: perform as a cost analyst responsible for controlling and analyzing all cost levels associated with a major plant in the DTI organization; explain unusual cost overruns; prepare a monthly cost forecast for a major plant and explain significant deviations from last month's forecast.	4 months
6. Financial Analysis: analyze and make recommendations on major capital expenditure proposals ($250,000 initial cash outlay and over); project net profit and cash flow (monthly and annually) by product line and plant; explain deviations from forecast.	5 months

For the past two weeks Jack Murray had gathered the financial data necessary to making an economically efficient choice between two models of chip crushers manufactured by Lamsden-Sexton, Inc. The higher cost model was identified by the code letters CCH (used in the production of fine scrap); the lower cost machine was noted by the code letters CCL (used in the production of rough scrap). Murray was to make a recommendation as to whether DTI should invest in CCH or CCL. It had previously been determined that one of the two chip crushers would be purchased.

As he entered the executive committee room, Murray immediately noticed one individual seated around the discussion table whom he had not expected to see in Des Moines on this Monday. That was Alex Longwood, sales manager for the Cuyahoga Falls Transmission and Axle Plant. Robert Lacy, the plant manager, was there as anticipated, but Longwood's presence puzzled Murray. He had an instant notion that any cause behind Longwood being at the DTI central office would not be favorable to the analysis about to be given the firm's officers and invited guests. Murray reflected upon his trip to Ohio some 10 days before and his final meeting with Lacy and Longwood. Although they had been most helpful in supplying him with needed information related to the purchase of either CCH or CCL, he somehow sensed that they were hoping his (Murray's) ultimate capital expenditure analysis would favor the purchase of CCL.

The investment outlay associated with CCH has been computed to be $480,000 versus a $400,000 outlay required for CCL. These estimates are firm quotes provided by Lamsden-Sexton, Inc., who would install the machine at no added cost. All of the investment outlay is to be depreciated on a straight line basis toward a zero estimated salvage value, over a 20-year economic life. In conjunction with the sales staff of Lamsden-Sexton, Inc. and the industrial engineering group located at the Transmission and Axle Plant, it was estimated that annual operating costs associated with CCH would be $480,00 and $250,000 for CCL. These costs are projected at a constant level over each of the next 20 years.

Alex Longwood supplied Jack Murray with the 20-year estimate of scrap revenues tied to each chip crusher. The fine scrap is expected to produce $800,000 per year in added sales, while the rough scrap is expected to add $500,000 annually to the sales total for DTI. Murray had these sales estimates checked by the central office marketing staff; that group felt the figures generated at the Ohio plant were reasonable. The DTI central office marketing people did impress upon Murray that the final sales outlet for the rough and fine steel scrap was largely concentrated in the Cleveland, Ohio, vicinity, less than an hour's drive from the Transmission and Axle Plant. Thus, the Ohio marketing group was considered expert on scrap revenue projections due to their proximity to the several buyers of the material.

For the past decade it has been established financial policy at DTI to evaluate possible capital expenditures using discounted cash flow techniques.

As an additional information item, the payback period is also computed. The corporate tax rate used for these analyses is 50 percent.

Murray's evaluation of the chip crusher project was the initial item on the agenda at this Monday's management meeting. He briefly described the nature of the project to the group, then he introduced William Clay, a sales representative from Lamsden-Sexton, Inc. Clay discussed the differing sales prices for CCH and CCL. He impressed upon the group that the investment cost of each machine was a firm quote including installation fees, as long as a purchase agreement was signed by both parties within the next 30 days. Murray then turned on the overhead slide projector and presented the key financial data and assumptions leading to his ultimate recommendation. His calculations reflected the fact that the office of the financial vice-president had issued a memorandum instructing the financial analysts to use a 14 percent cost of capital in all of their capital expenditure analyses during the next quarter of the year. Exhibits 2, 3, and 4 form the main elements of Murray's presentation.

EXHIBIT 2

Davidson Tractor and Implement

Chip Crusher Project: Cash Flow Projections

	CCH	CCL
Annual scrap revenues (net)	$800,000	$500,000
less change in operating costs	480,000	250,000
less change in depreciation	24,000	20,000
Change in taxable income	$296,000	$230,000
less change in tax at 50%	148,000	115,000
Change in after-tax profits	$148,000	$115,000
plus change in depreciation	24,000	20,000
Change in annual net cash flow (assumed constant for each of next 20 years)	$172,000	$135,000

Murray began by referring to Exhibit 2 and explaining the assumptions and company policies inherent to it. His objective, here, was to highlight clearly the uncertainties associated with the projection of net cash flows tied to each chip crusher. This was done by stating who was responsible within the DTI organization for supplying the key estimates displayed in Exhibit 2. The sales revenues, as mentioned earlier, were estimated by Alex Longwood's department at the Ohio plant. Again, the operating cost inputs were the joint effort of Lamsden-Sexton representatives and the Ohio plant's industrial engineering department. The tax rate and depreciation method used in derivation of the cash flows were set by company policy. For each of the next 20 years the net

EXHIBIT 3

Davidson Tractor and Implement

Chip Crusher Project: Internal Rates of Return

Part A: Analysis of CCH

Change in Annual Net Cash Flow	20-Year Annuity Factor at 35% and 36%	Present Value at 35% and 36%
$172,000	2.8501 (35%)	$490,217 (35%)
172,000	2.7718 (36%)	476,750 (36%)

Interpolation: $\dfrac{\$490,217 - 480,000}{490,217 - 476,750} = \dfrac{\$10,217}{13,467} = .76$

The internal rate of return is, therefore, 35.76%.

Part B: Analysis of CCL

Change in Annual Net Cash Flow	20-Year Annuity Factor at 33% and 34%	Present Value at 33% and 34%
$135,000	3.0202 (33%)	$407,727 (33%)
135,000	2.9327 (34%)	395,915 (34%)

Interpolation: $\dfrac{\$407,727 - 400,000}{407,727 - 395,915} = \dfrac{\$7,727}{11,812} = .65$

The internal rate of return is, therefore, 33.65%.

cash flows associated with the more expensive chip crusher were estimated at $172,000; the less costly machine was expected to generate cash flows of $135,000 per year over the same period.

Next, Murray focused the group's attention upon Exhibits 3 and 4. These tabulations contained the various measures of investment worth favored by the DTI organization. Murray pointed out that all of the time-adjusted evaluation methods that he had calculated (internal rate of return, net present value, and profitability index) favored investment in machine CCH, the more costly of the mutually exclusive alternatives. Even the payback period of CCH was expected to be faster than that of CCL. While observing that both projects were profitable if considered independent of each other, Murray reminded the group that only one could be purchased. He concluded that it made economic sense to spend the extra $80,000 and acquire CCH.

"Jack, do your revenue figures take into consideration the fact that DTI

EXHIBIT 4

Davidson Tractor and Implement

Chip Crusher Project: Net Present Values,
Profitability Indexes, and Payback Periods

Part A: Analysis of CCH

Change in Annual Net Cash Flow	20-Year Annuity Factor at 14%	Present Value at 14%
$172,000	6.6231	$1,139,173
	less investment outlay	480,000
	net present value	$ 659,173

Profitability index = $\dfrac{\$1,139,173}{480,000}$ = 2.37

Payback period = $\dfrac{\$480,000}{172,000}$ = 2.79 years[1]

Part B: Analysis of CCL

Change in Annual Net Cash Flow	20-Year Annuity Factor at 14%	Present Value at 14%
$135,000	6.6231	$894,119
	less investment outlay	400,000
	net present value	$494,119

Profitability index = $\dfrac{\$894,119}{400,000}$ = 2.24

Payback period = $\dfrac{\$400,000}{135,000}$ = 2.96 years

[1]Can be computed directly as projected net cash flows are even throughout economic life of the project.

would generate some scrap sales regardless of whether we bought either machine?"

That question came from Daniel Jenkens, vice-president for marketing. Murray had anticipated it. "Yes," he replied. "I used the term, net, in the exhibit where the scrap figures are estimated to indicate that only the excess above what DTI would generate without any new machine purchase has been analyzed."

"Fine," replied Jenkins; then he continued. "Over the weekend Bob Lacy and Alex Longwood called me to discuss some new information that I think will have to be incorporated into your computations. Since Alex is better versed on the material than I am, I've asked him to make a few comments to you and the rest of the management group."

Horrible Monday, Murray thought to himself, here it comes.

Longwood began. "Since Jack visited our plant a little over a week ago to gather inputs to this analysis, we have had to reassess the sales estimates supplied to him. New contracts let out and agreed upon during the past week with the several dealers in the Cleveland area who buy our processed scrap all indicate that future revenues of the type being discussed today will be lower than we had anticipated."

"Low enough to affect Jack's final recommendation to buy CCH?" asked Ronald Davidson, president of DTI.

"We're not sure," Bob Lacy answered. "We would like Jack to incorporate the newer sales estimates into his evaluation procedure, and then discuss the implications with this group."

Murray looked at Lacy and Longwood. "What are the new sales figures?" he asked.

Longwood flipped through a file folder in front of him and began, "For CCH we believe that $750,000 per year is more accurate, and for CCL we recommend use of $480,000 per year as the revenue projection." Longwood went on. "If this should alter the conclusion from your initial analysis, we have a proposal in the wings back in Cuyahoga Falls that promises an internal rate of return of around 17 to 18 percent on an $80,000 required investment outlay."

All of a sudden, things appeared clearer to Jack Murray. Lacy and Longwood were opting for the lower priced chip crusher in hopes of gaining use of the $80,000 price differential for investment in another project at their own plant.

Ronald Davidson turned to Jenkins and asked, "Do you think the new sales figures are firm enough to warant Jack running through his analysis again?"

"Yes."

"All right," said Davidson. "Jack, I want you to rework your computations and report back to this group immediately after lunch, at 1:00 p.m."

QUESTIONS

1. Compute all measures of investment worth (internal rate of return, net present value, profitability index, and payback period) originally calculated by Murray, but reflect the new sales projections in your analysis.

2. Is the solution as straightforward as it was when Murray made his initial presentation to the DTI management group?

3. Which chip crusher (CCH or CCL) would you recommend that DTI purchase?

Case 2

DANFORTH & DONNALLEY LAUNDRY PRODUCTS COMPANY

(Capital Budgeting: Relevant Cash Flows)

On April 14, 1973, at 3:00 p.m., James Danforth, president of Danforth & Donnalley (D & D) Laundry Products Company, called to order a meeting of the financial directors. The purpose of the meeting was to make a capital budgeting decision with respect to the introduction and production of a new product, a liquid detergent called Blast.

D & D was formed in 1955 with the merger of Danforth Chemical Company - headquartered in Seattle, Washington, producers of Lift-Off detergent, the leading laundry detergent on the West Coast - and Donnalley Home Products Company - headquartered in Detroit, Michigan, makers of Wave detergent, a major midwestern laundry product. As a result of the merger, D & D was producing and marketing two major product lines. Although these products were in direct competition, they were not without product differentiation; Lift-Off was a low suds, concentrated powder, and Wave was a more traditional powder detergent. Each line brought with it considerable brand loyalty, and, by 1973, sales from the two detergent lines had increased tenfold from their 1955 levels with both products now being sold nationally.

In the face of increased competition and technological innovation, D & D spent large amounts of time and money over the past four years researching and developing a new, highly concentrated liquid laundry detergent. D & D's new detergent, which they called Blast, had many obvious advantages over the conventional powdered products. It was felt that with Blast the consumer would benefit in three major areas. Blast was so highly concentrated that only two ounces was needed to do an average load of laundry as compared with 8 to 12 ounces of powdered detergent. Moreover, being a liquid, it was possible to pour Blast directly on stains and hard-to-wash spots, eliminating the need for a pre-soak and giving it cleaning abilities that powders could not possibly match. And, finally, it would be packaged in a lightweight, unbreakable plastic bottle with a sure-grip handle, making it much easier to use and more convenient to store than the bulky boxes of powdered detergents with which it would compete.

The meeting was attended by James Danforth, president of D & D; Jim Donnalley, director of the board; Guy Rainey, vice-president in charge of new products; Urban McDonald, controller; and Steve Gasper, a newcomer to D & D's financial staff, who was invited by McDonald to sit in on the meeting. Danforth called the meeting to order, gave a brief statement of its purpose, and immediately gave the floor to Guy Rainey.

Rainey opened with a presentation of the cost and cash flow analysis for the new product. To keep things clear, he passed out copies of the projected cash flows to those present (see Exhibits 1 and 2). In support of this information, he provided some insight as to how these calculations were determined. Rainey proposed that the initial cost for Blast included $500,000 for the test marketing, which was conducted in the Detroit area and completed in the previous June, and $2 million for new specialized equipment and pack-

EXHIBIT 1

Annual Cash Flows From the Acceptance of Blast

(Including those flows resulting from sales diverted from the existing product lines)

Year 1	$280,000
2	280,000
3	280,000
4	280,000
5	280,000
6	350,000
7	350,000
8	350,000
9	350,000
10	350,000
11	250,000
12	250,000
13	250,000
14	250,000
15	250,000

aging facilities. The estimated life for the facilities was 15 years, after which they would have no salvage value. This 15-year estimated life assumption coincides with company policy set by Donnalley not to consider cash flows occurring more than 15 years into the future, as estimates that far ahead "tend to become little more than blind guesses."

Rainey cautioned against taking the annual cash flows (as shown in Exhibit 1) at face value since portions of these cash flows actually are a result of sales that had been diverted from Lift-Off and Wave. For this reason, Rainey also produced the annual cash flows that had been adjusted to include only those cash flows incremental to the company as a whole (as shown in Exhibit 2).

At this point, discussion opened between Donnalley and McDonald, and it was concluded that the opportunity cost on funds is 10 percent. Gasper then questioned the fact that no costs were included in the proposed cash budget for plant facilities, which would be needed to produce the new product.

Rainey replied that, at the present time, Lift-Off's production facilities were being utilized at only 55 percent of capacity, and since these facilities were suitable for use in the production of Blast, no new plant facilities other than the specialized equipment and packaging facilities previously mentioned need be acquired for the production of the new product line. It was estimated that full production of Blast would only require 10 percent of the plant capacity.

McDonald then asked if there had been any consideration of increased working capital needs to operate the investment project. Rainey answered that

EXHIBIT 2

Annual Cash Flows From the Acceptance of Blast

(Not including those flows resulting from sales diverted from existing product lines)

Year 1	$250,000
2	250,000
3	250,000
4	250,000
5	250,000
6	315,000
7	315,000
8	315,000
9	315,000
10	315,000
11	225,000
12	225,000
13	225,000
14	225,000
15	225,000

there had and that this project would require $200,000 in additional working capital; however, as this money would never leave the firm and always would be in liquid form, it was not considered as outflow, hence, not included in the calculations.

Donnalley argued that this project should be charged something for its use of the current excess plant facilities. His reasoning was that if an outside firm tried to rent this space from D & D, they would be charged somewhere in the neighborhood of $2 million, and since this project will compete with the current projects, it should be treated as an outside project and charged as such. Otherwise, he concluded, they might end up accepting projects that under normal circumstances would be rejected.

From here, the discussion continued, centering itself on the questions of what to do about the "lost contribution from other projects," the test marketing costs, and the working capital.

QUESTIONS

1. If you were put in the place of Steve Gasper, would you argue for the cost from market testing to be included as a cash outflow?

2. What would your opinion be as to how to deal with the question of working capital?

3. Would you suggest that the product be charged for the use of excess production facilities and building? Would this opinion change if you knew that needed production facilities for the current line of powdered detergents was at 55 percent of capacity, maximum production capacity is 100 percent and expected to grow at a rate of 20 percent a year? What would be the present value of this cash flow given the fact that the currently proposed new plant will involve cash outflows of $5 million in three years (assume acceptance of the Blast project will not affect the size of the proposed outlay, only the timing, and that the new plant and facilities will be operable indefinitely). (Hint: Assume that the introduction of Blast will only move the need for a new plant ahead by one year and that the cash outflow will remain at $5 million regardless of when incurred, and that the plant will operate indefinitely.)

4. Would you suggest that the cash flows resulting from erosion of sales from current laundry detergent products be included as a cash inflow? If there was a chance of a <u>competition</u> introducing a similar product, would this affect your answer?

5. If debt is used to finance this project, should the interest payments associated with this new debt be considered cash flows?

6. What is the NPV, IRR, and PI of this project, including cash flows resulting from lost sales from existing product lines? What is the NPV, IRR, and PI of this project excluding these flows? Under the assumption that there is a good chance that competition will introduce a similar product, would you accept or reject this project?

Case 3

REDSTONE HEAT TREATING INCORPORATED

(Capital Budgeting: Depreciation Methods)

Redstone Heat Treating Incorporated (RHT) is located in Redstone, Michigan. The firm was started in 1947 by William D. Pierce, who at that time was 27 years old and had just been discharged from the Army Corps of Engineers. Pierce grew up in the metropolitan area that surrounds Detroit, Michigan, and holds a masters degree in mechanical engineering from a large midwestern university. He recognized that the auto industry would experience substantial growth following World War II, so he decided to take his chances and open his own plant, and at the same time take advantage of his engineering talents. Thus, RHT was born and soon became one of the many well-respected smaller firms that help to support the major automobile manufacturers concentrated in the Detroit area.

RHT provides heat treating processes for several different types of metals used in the final assembly of most American cars. Due to the problems of high temperatures and severe friction to which the moving parts of the automobile are subjected, the metals formed from such parts must be "hardened" prior to the machined parts being placed into their proper spot in the automobile mechanism. This type of business activity is characterized by its high level of capital intensity. The major assets of the firm, apart from the single-story building in which the operation is centered, are two huge heat treating furnaces, several fork lifts to move the parts being hardened around the plant, and a fleet of six trucks to pick up the "green" parts from the customer and to deliver them in hardened form back to the proper client.

Recently a major economic downturn has severely affected the automobile industry, and the unfavorable consequences of that recession have been transmitted to the suppliers of services and parts to the dominant producers. The resulting strain on both cash flow and profits has caused William Pierce, as president of RHT, to give extraordinary attention to the possible benefits of suggested asset purchases.

The day-to-day financial operations of RHT are handled by Charles Pierce, the son of the company president. The younger Pierce is active in the administration of the local chapter of the National Association of Corporate Cost Analysts (NACCA). Last month, after some friendly family arm twisting, Charles Pierce persuaded his father to attend with him a two-day seminar sponsored by the NACCA dealing with capital expenditure analysis. The son noted that the out-of-pocket cost of the seminar for both of them would be only $350. Given the critical nature of effective project analysis to RHT, the time away from the firm to attend the two-day session would be well spent; in addition, the $350 cost would be tax deductible to the firm. The younger man's main hope was that, after attending the seminar, his father would be more sympathetic to a requirement that major asset purchases be subjected to a detailed, discounted cash-flow type of analysis. Although the president of RHT knew full well the importance of effective economic studies of proposed asset purchases, he had often become irritated when his son used terms such as "net present value" and "internal rate of return" in their discussions of possible courses of company action. Charles Pierce realized that his father simply was not attuned to the jargon of contemporary financial management, and that the short introduction to capital budgeting techniques being sponsored by the local NACCA chapter would go a long way toward removal of the wall of unfamiliarity that stood between the son's favored methods of analysis and those typically used by the father in assessing project benefits.

A week after the seminar, Charles Pierce knew that his plan had succeeded. A four-hour meeting called by the president had just concluded. In addition to William and Charles Pierce, present at the lengthy session were Lawrence Jamison and George Willmot. Jamison is largely responsible for the firm's production scheduling; Willmot is the floor supervisor in charge of materials handling. For several years Jamison and Willmot had complained to William Pierce that the smaller heat treating jobs actually "robbed" the firm of profits. The hardening process for a few hundred gears, as an example, was essentially identical to that for an order of several hundred thousand. The small order, however, might have to be processed at a different oven temperature than the order just removed from the furnace; thus, production time was lost as the oven temperature was either raised or lowered. RHT had always been committed to a high level of company service, and accepted the small, specialty orders as well as the more profitable large orders. In his regular reading of trade magazines, Jamison noticed a new product was available for immediate delivery that might help to alleviate the production problem that plagued RHT. He brought it to the attention of the older Pierce.

At the meeting Jamison described in detail the benefits of the new product as they had been presented to him earlier in the week by a sales representative of the firm that produced the item. A smaller, more efficient furnace was now available for use in the basic heat treating process. It required less power to operate than its larger counterparts and adjusted to a wider range of internal oven temperatures at a faster rate than any other product previously available. The purchase price of the furnace, including installation charges, would be $260,000.

William Pierce and Lawrence Jamison worked up a forecast of the increased sales that would result from having the new oven available. This information is contained in Exhibit 1.

EXHIBIT 1

Projected Sales Increases
New Furnace Project

Years	Sales Increases
1	$130,000
2	300,000
3	270,000
4	150,000
5	150,000
6	150,000
7	120,000
8	80,000
9	80,000
10	60,000

It was estimated by Jamison and Willmot that cash operating costs associated with the project would amount to only 10 percent of the projected sales increases each year. While the asset would in all likelihood be useful to the firm beyond a 10-year period, it would be depreciated over that life toward a zero estimated salvage value. It was also agreed that no sales increases would be forecast beyond the 10-year depreciable life of the oven.

Charles Pierce related to the others at the meeting that he had calculated the firm's cost of capital to be in the area of 12 percent and would use that estimate in this project analysis. He further noted that the firm for several years had experienced an average tax rate of about 48 percent. He argued that he would prefer to use the double declining balance method of depreciating the asset for the first five years of its life, with a switch occuring to the straight line method after the fifth year. Even though William Pierce had attended the recent capital budgeting seminar with his son, he was somewhat curious as to the advantage of the depreciation technique that Charles had outlined. The president concluded this phase of the project examination by assigning his son the responsibility for performing a complete financial analysis of the possible benefits related to the purchase of the new furnace.

QUESTIONS

1. Prepare depreciation expense schedules for the project using (a) straight line, (b) double declining balance, and (c) double declining balance with a switch to straight line at the end of the fifth year.

2. Using the depreciation approach favored by Charles Pierce, calculate (a) the internal rate of return, (b) the net present value, and (c) the profitability index for the proposed investment.

3. Using the information developed in question 2, calculate the project (a) payback period and (b) average rate of return.

4. To demonstrate clearly the advantage of the depreciation technique suggested by Charles Pierce, use straight line depreciation and calculate (a) the internal rate of return, (b) the net present value, and (c) the profitability index for the proposed investment.

5. Comment on your overall findings and point out whether or not RHT should purchase the new furnace.

Case 4

UNITED TECHNIQUES, INC.

(Capital Budgeting: Partially Dependent Cash Flows)

Profits for United Techniques, Inc. (UTI) declined over the past year as a result of the hard times that befell the construction industry during 1974-1975. UTI manufactures laser components used in the production of laser based transits, which now have largely replaced the traditional optical transit. In 1975, UTI earned $2 million, or 60 cents per share on sales of $34.2 million, down from $2.7 million, or 79 cents per share in fiscal 1974.

The laser was first developed in 1960, but has found very little practical use until recently. Presently, lasers are being used in a wide array of applications ranging from cleaning devices to high speed, computer printout machines and full-color copying machines. One of the more promising areas for profitable investment in the industry lies in point of sale (POS) checkout equipment for supermarkets. In an effort to diversify its product offerings and to revive the sales momentum that the company experienced during the early part of the 1970s, UTI is considering the possibility of developing and marketing its own POS checkout system.

With the POS system, checkers in supermarkets simply pass the customer's merchandise over a small window in the checkout stand where the laser is used to read a code imprinted on the boxes and cans. The code (actually a sequence of bars of various widths) simply identifies the item being "rung up." The register can then search its memory for the price of the item and add it to the customer's bill. Simultaneously, as the customer's purchases are being checked, the store's inventory is altered to reflect the sale. The improved checkout system is expected to reduce supermarket labor costs substantially, as well as making possible more precise inventory control.

UTI's management has investigated the possiblities for entry into the POS checkout system market and finds that it has two basic alternatives. The firm can produce the system on a contract basis for a major supplier of cash registers and other checkout equipment, or it can produce and market its own system. If the former alternative is selected, the firm can contract with National Registers, Inc., to produce its optical scanning equipment for a two-year period and for a contract valued at an expected $10 million. At the end of the contract period, UTI has the option to rebid another contract or it may decide at that time to market its own POS system. Marketing its own POS system would, of course, entail the assumption of all the risks involved in such a venture. Also, if the firm chooses this alternative, it will not be able to accept the National Register contract.

Jim Reynolds, UTI's financial vice-president, called a special meeting of the firm's finance committee to consider the proposed investment. The primary issue discussed was just how to handle the "multiple" and "sequential" decisions involved 'in making the investment decision. Specifically, it appears that UTI has three possible courses of action: (1) the firm can market its own POS system from the outset, (2) it can contract with National Register to produce its line of POS equipment and attempt to rebid the contract at the end of the two-year period (UTI's management feels confident that it could successfully rebid the contract if it so desires), or (3) the firm can take the National Register contract for two years with the idea of offering its own product line at the end of that period. Each of the alternatives has its own merits and dangers. Relevant project net present values (NPV's) for each course of action, as well as three levels of projected product demand, are presented in Exhibit 1. Probabilities have been "subjectively" attached to each possible set of outcomes or events, which in turn consist of both the decisions and chance events that characterize the investment proposition. The three demand levels used by UTI's analysts in developing the information necessary to the analysis of the alternatives correspond to "optimistic," "most likely," and "pessimistic" forecasts of what the future will produce in the way of project returns.

Reynolds has asked that the analysts limit their return forecasts to a 10-year horizon based on both the "gross uncertainties" that surround the project returns and the very real possibility that strong competition will quickly develop should the POS equipment really catch hold.

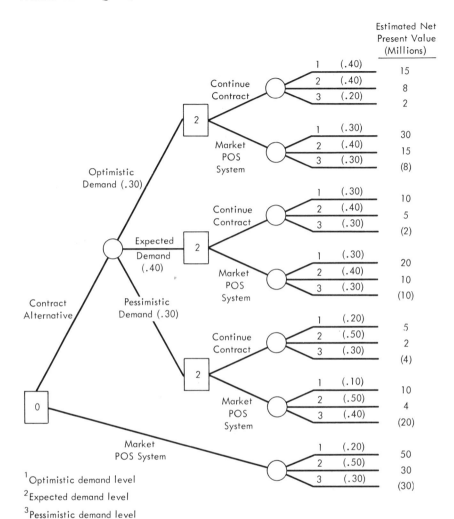

Estimated Net
Present Value
(Millions)

Continue Contract — 1 (.40) 15, 2 (.40) 8, 3 (.20) 2

Market POS System — 1 (.30) 30, 2 (.40) 15, 3 (.30) (8)

Optimistic Demand (.30)

Continue Contract — 1 (.30) 10, 2 (.40) 5, 3 (.30) (2)

Expected Demand (.40)

Market POS System — 1 (.30) 20, 2 (.40) 10, 3 (.30) (10)

Contract Alternative   Pessimistic Demand (.30)

Continue Contract — 1 (.20) 5, 2 (.50) 2, 3 (.30) (4)

Market POS System — 1 (.10) 10, 2 (.50) 4, 3 (.40) (20)

Market POS System — 1 (.20) 50, 2 (.50) 30, 3 (.30) (30)

[1]Optimistic demand level

[2]Expected demand level

[3]Pessimistic demand level

EXHIBIT 1

QUESTIONS

1. Analyze the firm's investment options with respect to the development of a POS checkout system. What is your recommendation as to the course of action that the firm should take?

2. If UTI should simultaneously face the prospect of making a "mutually exclusive" investment with an expected net present value [E(NPV)] of $20,000,000 and a standard deviation in NPV [S(NPV)] of $14,000,000, which alternative would you recommend? What would you recommend should the alternative investment have an E(NPV) = $20,000,000 and S(NPV) = $22,000,000?

Case 5

CONTINENTAL MOTORS CORPORATION

(Capital Budgeting: Probability Distributions)

After 60 years of operation, Continental Motors Corporation (CMC) is facing its second major crisis. The company's first crisis occurred in 1946 following World War II, when it had to reconvert outdated tank production facilities back into automobile production facilities. Now, its second major crisis, a dramatic cutback in sales, has apparently been caused by the economic downturn of 1974-75 and changes in the American public's attitude toward large size cars resulting from the increased cost of gasoline and heightened pollution concerns.

The early history of CMC is essentially the biography of its founder, David Dorner. In his youth, Dorner became very interested in the gasoline combustion engine and conducted many experiments with it before entering the mechanical engineering school at Purdue University in 1909. During his years at Purdue, Dorner continued his experiments, working closely with a classmate, Gene Alexander, and upon graduation these two young men went into business as Dorner Alexander Engines Incorporated, located in Frankfort, Indiana. Within a year Dorner had applied for over 15 major patents and within two years began producing engines for race cars. Shortly after Dorner branched out on his own, forming CMC for the production of racing and sports cars.

Between 1916 and 1925, while the number of competitors in the automobile industry increased, the number of models marketed by CMC grew from 2 to 12, primarily through acquisition. Still, as CMC expanded its product line, it stayed within the area of smaller cars emphasizing production excellence. During this period, and up until the outbreak of World War II, CMC continued to grow at a moderate pace in spite of the unfavorable economic conditions of the '30s. However, with the outbreak of World War II, CMC virtually ceased production of automobiles and began production of tanks and airplanes needed for the war effort. At the end of the war, CMC faced its first major crisis when Dorner found himself in a difficult position with production facilities that were by then deteriorating and a product line that had not been changed since early 1941. During the next two years, CMC suffered large losses and was kept alive only by tax refunds from loss carry-backs. New production facilities were built during this period, and by 1948 CMC had introduced an entirely new line of automobiles, focusing on the small, low priced car, which had come to be called the compact car, still stressing the excellent engineering that had been the trademark of CMC.

The period from 1948 to 1974 was marked by strong cyclical growth with sales peaks coming about every five years. During this time period CMC's sales reached a peak of $2.8 billion in 1973. However, in the second half of 1974 and 1975, CMC's sales dropped to about 57 percent of this level, creating the company's second major crisis. This drop in sales was a result of several factors working in combination. First, antipollution features were becoming standard on the 1975 line of automobiles, which were first marketed in late 1974. These features were expected to raise the base sticker price of automobiles from $500 to $800 each. The result was that many new car customers, who normally would have waited until the 1975 models were introduced to purchase a new automobile, bought 1974 models in an attempt to avoid paying for anti-pollution devices. Moreover, new car customers who did not purchase 1974 models began postponing planned purchases of 1975 models, because of the rapid rise in new car costs. This fact both complicated and was complicated by the recession that broke out in early 1974. The drop in new car buying caused a further deepening in the recession, which in turn weakened consumer confidence causing further postponement of new car purchases. As if this were not enough, the sharp increase in the price of foreign oil, which caused a doubling in the price of gasoline over this period, made new car buyers increasingly concerned with gasoline efficiency. Unfortunately, although CMC did produce smaller, low priced cars, they were not particularly fuel efficient, and increased competition trom domestic car makers and foreign imports caused a further weakening of CMC's hold on the small car market.

The cumulative result of these factors was that CMC's existence was actually being challenged. Its 1974-75 losses forbade the raising of large sums of money in the capital market that were desperately needed to reverse this situation. As a result, CMC, which is currently considering four major capital investments, each with a 10-year life, must limit its selection to only one of these projects.

Project A is the development and introduction of a new small to medium-size luxury car to compete directly with the foreign-made Audi. Management feels that this new car will fill the current demand for a luxury car for consumers not willing to pay from $8,000 to $12,000. This car would provide new sales for CMC in addition to attracting new customers to CMC showrooms, which management feels would likely result in an increase in sales of the existing line. The cash flows associated with this proposal are shown in Exhibit 1.

Investment project B involves the development and introduction of a wide-bodied compact car. This new car will have more glass than other cars on the market. The result will be a distinctive appearance, unlike any other car currently available. Marketing surveys have shown that this glassed-in look, in addition to the wide wheel base, are two factors desired by economy-minded automobile customers but unavailable at the present time. It is expected that this new entry into the auto market will provide the comfort and front seat space of a luxury car with a base sticker price of about $3,000. The cash flows associated with this proposal are given in Exhibit 1.

The development of a four cylinder engine for use in CMC's smaller compact and subcompact cars is proposed in project C. Currently CMC does not have a four cylinder or a six cylinder engine efficient enough to deliver the fuel economy to be competitive with that delivered by the foreign subcompacts. The problem of inefficient engines has hurt CMC severely and the possibility of remedying this situation has drawn much support from upper levels of CMC management. The cash flows associated with this proposal are given in Exhibit 1.

The final investment proposal, project D, involves the modernization of a Detroit assembly plant. This is the oldest plant currently being operated by CMC; it was built during 1940-41 and immediately converted into an assembly plant for B-24 bombers. After the war, the plant was reconverted for use in the production of automobiles, but since then has begun to show increasing signs of aging as reflected in mounting breakdowns. Because of CMC's five-year buyer protection warranty covering all parts and labor, except those breakdowns or malfunctions resulting from delinquent care or accidents, CMC has become increasingly concerned about the operation of this plant. It seems that while it produces only 17 percent of CMC's output, 31 percent of all the warranty claims on workmanship come on cars produced at this plant. The cash flows associated with this proposal also are given in Exhibit 1.

QUESTIONS

1. What are the expected cash flows associated with each project?
2. Calculate the net present value, profitability index, and internal rate of return for each project. Use 10 percent as the cost of capital.

EXHIBIT 1

Initial Outflow

Project A		Project B	
Probability	Cash Outflow	Probability	Cash Outflow
1.00	10,000,000	1.00	10,000,000

Project C		Project D	
Probability	Cash Outflow	Probability	Cash Outflow
.02	9,000,000	.03	8,000,000
.96	10,000,000	.47	9,500,000
.02	11,000,000	.47	10,500,000
		.03	12,000,000

Annual Cash Inflows
(Constant for years 1-10, no flows
anticipated for any project after year 10.)

Project A		Project B	
Probability	Cash Inflow	Probability	Cash Inflow
.03	2,200,000	.05	2,000,000
.47	2,800,000	.10	2,500,000
.47	3,200,000	.35	3,000,000
.03	3,800,000	.35	3,200,000
		.10	3,700,000
		.05	4,200,000

Project C		Project D	
Probability	Cash Inflow	Probability	Cash Inflow
.03	2,200,000	.07	1,200,000
.07	2,800,000	.16	1,800,000
.80	3,000,000	.40	3,500,000
.07	3,200,000	.32	3,700,000
.03	3,800,000	.05	3,800,000

3. Should the cost of capital used in the calculations in question 2 be the same for each project? Why?

4. What is the standard deviation on Project A? On projects B, C, and D, the standard deviation is $447,214, $209,762, and $851,284, respectively; What is the coefficient of variation on each project?

5. Is the use of the standard deviation or coefficient of variation appropriate in the evaluation of project D? Why? (Hint: Examine the normality of the distribution of returns for project D.)

6. How would the correlation between the expected returns of different projects, and the existing operations of the firm, affect the total risk parameter of the firm?

7. How might dependence of cash flows over time affect the overall risk of a project?

Case 6

HARDING PLASTIC MOLDING COMPANY

(Capital Budgeting: Ranking Problems)

On January 11, 1975, the finance committee of Harding Plastic Molding Company (HPMC) met to consider eight capital budgeting projects. Present at the meeting were Robert L. Harding, president and founder, Susan Jorgensen, comptroller, and Chris Woelk, head of research and development. Over the past five years this committee has met every month to consider and make final judgment on all proposed capital outlays brought up for review during the period.

Harding Plastic Molding Company was founded in 1954 by Robert L. Harding to produce plastic parts and molding for the Detroit automakers. For the first 10 years of operations, HPMC worked solely as a subcontractor for the automakers, but since then has made strong efforts to diversify in an attempt to avoid the cyclical problems faced by the auto industry. By 1970 this diversification attempt had led HPMC into the production of over 1,000 different items, including kitchen utensils, camera housings, phonographic and recording equipment. It also led to an increase in sales of 500 percent during the 1964 to 1974 period. As this dramatic increase in sales was paralleled by a corresponding increase in production volume, HPMC was forced, in late 1973, to expand production facilities. This plant and equipment expansion involved capital expenditures of approximately $10.5 million and resulted in an increase of production capacity of about 40 percent. Because of this increased production capacity,

HPMC has made a concerted effort to attract new business, and, consequently, has recently entered into contracts with a large toy firm and a major discount department store chain. While nonauto related business has grown significantly, it still only represents 32 percent of HPMC's overall business. Thus, HPMC has continued to solicit nonautomotive business, and as a result of this effort and its internal research and development, the firm has four sets of mutually exclusive projects to consider at this month's finance committee meeting.

Over the past 10 years, HPMC's capital budgeting approach has evolved into a somewhat elaborate procedure in which new proposals are categorized into three areas; profit, research and development, and safety. Projects falling into the profit or research and development area are evaluated using present value techniques, assuming a 10 percent opportunity rate; those falling into the safety classification are evaluated in a more subjective framework. Although research and development projects have to receive favorable results from the present value criteria, there is also a total dollar limit assigned to projects of this category, typically running about $750,000 per year. This limitation was imposed by Harding primarily because of the limited availability of quality researchers in the plastics industry. Harding felt that if more funds than this were allocated, "we simply couldn't find the manpower to administer them properly." The benefits derived from safety projects, on the other hand, are not in terms of cash flows, hence present value methods are not used at all in their evaluation. The subjective approach used to evaluate safety projects is a result of the pragmatically difficult task of quantifying the benefits from these projects into dollar terms. Thus, these projects are subjectively evaluated by a management-worker committee with a limited budget. All eight projects to be evaluated in January are classified as profit projects.

The first set of projects listed on the meeting's agenda for examination involve the utilization of HPMC's precision equipment. Project A calls for the production of vacuum containers for thermos bottles produced for a large discount hardware chain. The containers would be manufactured in five different size and color combinations. This project would be carried out over a three-year period, for which HPMC would be guaranteed a minimum return plus a percentage of the sales. Project B involves the manufacture of inexpensive photographic equipment for a national photography outlet. Although HPMC currently has excess plant capacity, both of these projects would utilize precision equipment of which the excess capacity is limited. Thus, adopting either project would tie up all precision facilities. In addition, the purchase of new equipment would be both prohibitively expensive and involve a time delay of approximately two years, thus making these projects mutually exclusive. (The cash flows associated with these two projects are given in Exhibit 1.)

The second set of projects involves the renting of computer facilities over a one-year period to aid in customer billing and perhaps inventory control. Project C entails the evaluation of a customer billing system proposed by Advanced Computer Corporation. Under this system, all of the bookkeeping and

EXHIBIT 1

Cash Flows

Year	Project A	Project B
0	$ -75,000	$-75,000
1	10,000	43,000
2	30,000	43,000
3	100,000	43,000

billing presently being done by HPMC's accounting department would now be done by Advanced. In addition to saving costs involved in bookkeeping, Advanced would provide a more efficient billing system and do a credit analysis of delinquent customers, which could be used in the future for in-depth credit analysis. Project D is proposed by International Computer Corporation and includes a billing system similar to that offered by Advanced, and, in addition, an inventory control system that will keep track of all raw materials and parts in stock, and reorder when necessary; thereby reducing the likelihood of material stockouts, which has become more and more frequent over the past three years. (The cash flows for these projects are given in Exhibit 2.)

EXHIBIT 2

Cash Flows

Year	Project C	Project D
0	$ -8,000	$-20,000
1	11,000	25,000

The third decision that faces the financial directors of HPMC involves a newly developed and patented process for molding hard plastics. HPMC can either manufacture and market the equipment necessary to mold such plastics or they can sell the patent rights to Polyplastics Incorporated, the world's largest producers of plastics products. (The cash flows for projects E and F are shown in Exhibit 3.) At present, the process has not been fully tested, and if HPMC is going to market it itself, it will be necessary to complete this testing and begin production of plant facilities immediately. On the other hand, the selling of these patent rights to Polyplastics would involve only minor testing and refinements, which could be completed within the year. Thus, a decision as to the proper course of action is necessary immediately.

The final set of projects up for consideration revolve around the replacement of some of the machinery. HPMC can go in one of two directions. Project G suggests the purchase and installation of moderately priced, extremely efficient equipment with an expected life of five years; project H advocates

EXHIBIT 3

Cash Flows

Year	Project E	Project F
0	$ -30,000	$-271,500
1	210,000	100,000
2		100,000
3		100,000
4		100,000
5		100,000
6		100,000
7		100,000
8		100,000
9		100,000
10		100,000

the purchase of a similarly priced, although less efficient machine with life expectancy of 10 years. (The cash flows for these alternatives are shown in Exhibit 4.)

EXHIBIT 4

Cash Flows

Year	Project G	Project H
0	$-500,000	$-500,000
1	225,000	150,000
2	225,000	150,000
3	225,000	150,000
4	225,000	150,000
5	225,000	150,000
6		150,000
7		150,000
8		150,000
9		150,000
10		150,000

As the meeting opened, debate immediately centered on the most appropriate method for evaluating all of the projects. Harding suggested that as the projects to be considered were mutually exclusive, perhaps their usual capital budgeting criteria of net present value was inappropriate. He felt that, in examining these projects, perhaps they should be more concerned with relative profitability of some measure of yield. Both Jorgensen and Woelk agreed with

Harding's point of view, with Jorgensen advocating a profitability index approach and Woelk preferring the use of the internal rate of return. Jorgensen argued that the use of the profitability index would provide a benefit-cost ratio, directly implying relative profitability. Thus, they merely need to rank these projects and select those with the highest profitability index. Woelk agreed with Jorgensen's point of view, but suggested that the calculation of an internal rate of return would also give a measure of profitability and perhaps be somewhat easier to interpret. To settle the issue, Harding suggested that they calculate all three measures, as they would undoubetdly yield the same ranking.

From here the discussion turned to an appropriate approach to the problem of differing lives among mutually exclusive projects E and F, and G and H. Woelk argued that there really was not a problem here at all, that as all of the cash flows from these projects can be determined, any of the discounted cash flow methods of capital budgeting will work well. Jorgensen, on the other hand, argued that although this was true, she felt that some compensation should be made for the fact that the projects being considered did not have equal lives.

QUESTIONS

1. Was Harding correct in stating that the NPV, PI, and IRR necessarily will yield the same ranking order? Under what situations might the NPV, PI, and IRR methods provide different rankings? Why is it possible?

2. What is the NPV, PI, and IRR for projects A and B? What has caused the ranking conflicts? Should project A or B be chosen? Might your answer change if project B is a typical project in the plastic molding industry? For example, if projects for HPMC generally yield approximately 12 percent, is it logical to assume that the IRR for project B of approximately 33 percent is a correct calculation for ranking purposes? (Hint: Examine the reinvestment assumption rate.)

3. What is the NPV, PI, and IRR for projects C and D? Should project C or D be chosen? Does your answer change if these projects are considered under a capital constraint? What return on the marginal $12,000 not employed in project C is necessary to make one indifferent between these projects under a capital rationing situation?

4. What is the NPV, PI, and IRR for projects E and F? Are these projects comparable even though they have unequal lives? Why? Which project should be chosen? Assume these projects are not considered under a capital constraint.

5. What is the NPV, PI, and IRR for projects G and H? Are these projects comparable even though they have unequal lives? Why? Which project should be chosen? Assume these projects are not considered under a capital contraint.

RON WILLINGHAM COURSES, INC.

(Capital Budgeting: Basic Difficulties)

Ron Willingham Courses, Inc., founded by Ron Willingham in 1972, has dealt primarily in personal and professional motivational courses particularly for corporate employees. Willingham and his associates have developed several programs that have proven successful in their reception by the individuals completing the courses.

At the present time, extensive thought and consideration are being committed to a new program to be used by banks and/or savings and loan institutions as a client service. The course material, entitled the MONY Plan, is addressed to the need and strategy for managing an individual's personal resources. In this regard, James Williams, the executive vice-president, has identified a strong potential market for such courses for both business executives actively involved in the management of large amounts of corporate funds as well as persons having little experience in the proper management of money. In visiting with the executives of various financial institutions, Williams has received several commitments to purchase the course. However, he is reluctant to initialize the sales campaign until additional investigation has been completed into the impact of several strategies upon the profitability of the firm. Specifically, questions still remain both in terms of the expected life of the instructional material and the marketing strategy.

In analyzing the prospects of the investment, Willingham and Williams consider the basic product to have an expected life of approximately five years (Plan A). However, this estimate could be significantly lengthened, provided either an extensive marketing campaign was conducted in subsequent years (Plan B below) or a major revision in the course package is developed in the fifth year (Plan C). In this regard, the options under consideration may be summarized as follows:

Plan A: This first strategy requires an investment at the present time totaling $300,000. This amount would afford the necessary funds for production equipment as well as working capital requirements of $50,000. The working capital portion of the investment may be liquidated upon the termination of the course. The expected life of the project is five years.

Plan B: The second alternative would permit an increase in the expected life of the course to 10 years. Based upon experience with prior investments of a similar type, the firm's management considers the feasibility of a project in terms of length of life to be quite sensitive to increased efforts in customer awareness in the latter years of the program. Thus, the extension of the product life would come from an intensive marketing campaign in years 6 through 10. The capital investment would be similar to the amount under Plan A in that the same capital expenditure would be made; however, $100,000 in working capital would have to be maintained, as opposed to only $50,000 for Plan A.

Plan C: The final analysis to be performed relates to a two-phase investment in which the initial capital investment of $350,000 is committed, including $100,000 in working capital, and $200,000 must be expended on equipment at the conclusion of the fifth year. This investment would result in substantive modifications and improvements in the program. While time is of essence in going to the market, within the next few years several major improvements in educational equipment is expected. Such a two-phase investment would permit receiving the benefits of these developments.

Succinctly stated, the management is considering two basic approaches for promoting MONY Plan: (1) a concentrated effort with the intent being to saturate the market during a 5-year period (Plan A) or (2) an extended investment in MONY Plan, with the prolonged life being the result of a marketing campaign in years 6 through 10 (Plan B) or a major revamping of the course structure in the fifth year (Plan C).

The estimates of the annual receipts and operational expenses for the three plans are given below.

Year	Sales		
	Plan A	Plan B	Plan C
1	$100,000	$ 75,000	$ 75,000
2	300,000	125,000	125,000
3	450,000	200,000	200,000
4	450,000	280,000	280,000
5	450,000	350,000	350,000
6		400,000	475,000
7		425,000	500,000
8		475,000	500,000
9		450,000	500,000
10		250,000	500,000

Year(s)	Marketing Expenses Per Year		
	Plan A	Plan B	Plan C
1-5	$35,000	$25,000	$25,000
6-7		50,000	25,000
8-9		70,000	25,000
10		25,000	25,000

Additional data thought to bear on the decision are:

1. The production of the material will require the use of a portion of an existing plant not included in the capital investment figures quoted above. This part of the plant, which represents excess floor space, could be considered to have a book value of $150,000 and a corresponding annual depreciation of $10,000 per year. However, this segment of the plant could not be used otherwise due to the floor plan of the building.

2. Cost of goods sold of similar programs has generally been a variable cost approximating 60 percent of sales.

3. Administrative expenses for the company will be $10,000 annually, which has been the level of administration expenses for the past year. However, only $4,000 of this amount will be allocated via the cost accounting system to the new plan.

4. The bank has agreed to finance $100,000 of the investment at an interest rate of 8 percent, with the interest being payable yearly and the principal coming due at the end of the project life.

5. The company is in a 40 percent tax rate and uses straight line depreciation (no salvage) for all expenditures.

QUESTIONS

1. Determine the costs of the three alternatives.
2. Compute the annual after-tax cash flows for the three plans.
3. Compute the net present value, the profitability index, and the internal rate of return for each plan, assuming a cost of capital of 8 percent.
4. Which course of action should be taken by the firm? Explain.

Case 8

SOUTHWESTERN COAL CORPORATION

(Capital Budgeting: The Risk-Adjusted Rate of Return and Certainty-Equivalent Approaches)

On December 31, 1977, the Southwestern Coal Corporation was investigating the feasibility of two mutually exclusive projects. The first prospective investment involved a strip mining operation in eastern Tennessee. The second investment also involved the extraction of coal, but this expenditure would be an underground site in southwestern Virginia.

For the past several months, Bill Jamison had been involved in the development of revenue and expense projections for the two projects. In his analysis, sufficient data existed from prior investments to provide relatively accurate cost data. After having drawn upon this information, Jamison made the following projections as to investment costs for each operation:

	Strip Mining	Underground Mining
Leasehold Investment	$ 400,000	$ 300,000
Equipment	3,000,000	1,500,000
Additional Working Capital Requirements	200,000	200,000
Total	$3,600,000	$2,000,000

With respect to these figures, experience suggests that a 10-year life may be expected on either of the two prospective investments, with the practice being to expense the leasehold investments on a straight line basis over the life. Furthermore, the equipment would be depreciated over the same life on a straight line basis. However, the projected salvage value for the strip mining operation would be $600,000, while the equipment for the underground plant could be expected to have a residual value of $150,000. The exigency for incremental working capital as a result of the investment would arise at the time of the investment, but could be released upon the termination of the project, with only a negligible chance of the full amount not being recovered.

In addition to the cost estimates, the engineers, based upon studies of the subsurface formations, were able to make projections as to the revenues that could be generated from the two fields. As a result of their studies, expected earnings after taxes for the two investments would be as follows:

	Years	Expected Earnings after Taxes per Year
Strip Mining:	1-4	$400,000.
	5-7	220,000.
	8-10	100,000.
Underground Mining:	1-4	$360,000.
	5-7	230,000.
	8-10	130,000.

Upon receiving the above information, Jamison questioned the reliability of the anticipated earnings. In response, Duane Proctor, head of the engineering staff at Southwestern Coal, informed him that both projects would have to be considered to be more risky than the firm's typical investment. Furthermore, the personnel conducting the analysis indicated that the expected cash flows from the underground mining operation were subject to considerably more uncertainty than the strip mining. In fact, Proctor considered the extraction of coal through the underground facility to be twice as risky as that of the strip mining alternative. For this reason, he recommended that the strip mining project be discounted at a 10 percent rate, while the underground mining proposal be analyzed with a 20 percent criteria. Jamison questioned Proctor's logic in that the company's cost of capital had been computed to be 8 percent. He believed this figure better reflected the stockholders' required rate of return, and for that reason should be used as the discount rate for both projects.

In support of his position concerning the riskiness of the two proposed investments, Proctor developed some in-depth work sheets for Jamison, which suggested other possible returns depending upon the amount of coal actually extracted from the mines. As a summary measurement of the possible deviations from the expected values, the engineering staff further calculated the standard deviation of the returns. These calculations are shown below:

	Years	Standard Deviation of Earnings after Taxes
Strip Mining:	1-4	$340,000
	5-7	250,000
	8-10	190,000
Underground Mining:	1-4	$315,000
	5-7	276,500
	8-10	236,000

In addition to the standard deviation of these reported earnings, the engineering personnel estimated the standard deviation relating to the salvage value of each project to be $300,000 for the strip mining facility and $135,000 for the underground mining equipment.

In reviewing the engineering department's work, Jamison was quite pleased with the results. However, a question remained in his mind as to the soundness of employing the various discount rates as suggested by Proctor. Jamison had been particularly interested in this question even before the two projects in question had been brought before him. As an alternative to adjusting the discount rate for dissimilar investments in terms of risk, he had been conducting some informal seminars with top management in the hopes of establishing a pattern of their attitude toward risk. From these sessions, he was able to specify the relationship between the level of risk and the willingness of management to accept such uncertainty, as reflected by "certainty-equivalent factors." The results of these meetings are depicted in Exhibit 1. With this information, he felt that a better approach would be to adjust the cash flows by the appropriate certainty-equivalent factor and to discount these adjusted flows at the firm's cost of capital. However, Proctor is of the opinion that the risk-free rate, which is currently 6 percent, would be more appropriate for such an analysis. At this point, the investigation has been temporarily halted until the questions confronting the men have been resolved.

QUESTIONS

1. Given both the expected values of returns and a measure of the risk accompanying these returns for two mutually exclusive projects, can an individual determine the better investment to accept? ("Better" is defined as the investment that may be identified as being unequivocably preferable for any decision maker.)
2. Specifically define the "certainty-equivalent factor." How does it differ from the probability of an event occurring?

EXHIBIT 1

Management's Risk-Return Profile

Coefficient of Variation[1]	Certainty-Equivalent Factor[2]
.5	.95
.6	.93
.7	.91
.8	.88
.9	.85
1.0	.82
1.1	.78
1.2	.74
1.3	.70
1.4	.64
1.5	.58
1.6	.52
1.7	.43
1.8	.33
1.9	.15

[1] The coefficient of variation is a relative measure of dispersion, calculated by dividing the standard deviation by the expected value.

[2] The factor states the amount management would accept for certain in lieu of $1 expected return.

3. As reflected in Exhibit 1, graph the relationship between risk and the certainty-equivalent factor. Would the company's management be considered to be risk seekers, risk neutral, or risk averters? Explain your answer.

4. a. Calculate the net present value for each investment employing (a) the certainty-equivalent approach and (b) the risk-adjusted rate of return method.

   b. Are the results of the certainty-equivalent methodology and the risk-adjusted rate approach consistent, that is, do both techniques indicate acceptance of the same project? If an inconsistency does exist, explain the reason(s) why.

5. Under what condition(s) should the decision maker use the risk-adjusted discount rate or an adjustment of cash flows by a certainty-equivalent factor as opposed to simply discounting the expected cash flows by the cost of capital?

6. a. Compute the necessary expected cash flows of an "average risk" asset that would be deemed equivalently acceptable to management as the underground mining operation when examined by the risk-adjusted rate of return.

   b. Set up the solution (but do not solve) for determining the risk-adjusted rate of return that would provide identical results as the certainty-equivalent approach for the strip mining project.

Case 9

UNIVERSITY CITY LOUNGE

(Capital Budgeting: Probability Distributions)

Richard James operates University City Lounge (UCL) as a small corporation in the college community of Claremont, Pennsylvania, about 65 miles north of Pittsburgh. Although it is primarily a university-oriented city, Claremont has a diversified and sound industrial base. In fact, the town's older residents like to boast that the community has never suffered a depression. James founded UCL five years ago in the downtown section of the city, which serves largely as the main retail outlet for the 10,000 students of Claremont State University. As other shopowners left the downtown area to move to newly constructed shopping centers on the outskirts of the city, James expanded his restaurant and lounge into the vacated, adjacent spaces. He enjoys a profitable operation. The net income from the business has grown by about 10 percent each year since its inception. James owns all of the stock of UCL.

James is 28 years old, a Navy veteran, and a high school graduate. The firm has no outstanding contractual debt. A one-year note that was taken at a local commercial bank to launch the business was repaid on a timely basis. James maintains good personal relations with several local bankers who frequent his restaurant and lounge operation; all of them are impressed with his hard work at the business.

The restaurant and lounge are organized to appeal to high school students, college students, and, in general, young adults. This is accomplished through

113

the maintenance of three separate environments within the space rented by James. The center of the business is a short-order food and drink service. The menu is brief and includes hot dogs, hamburgers, pizza, sliced beef sandwiches, fried shrimp, soft drinks, and beer. The room that houses this aspect of the business contains 10 tables that seat 4 persons each and 5 large booths that hold 6 persons each. Waitresses are employed to serve customers only in this area of the UCL.

A separate game room to the left (with respect to the entrance) of the main eating area contains 2 air hockey tables, 6 pinball machines, and 2 bar-sized pool tables. There are 5 tables that seat 20 customers in total in the game room, so that food and drink are readily consumed in the area. The appeal of this aspect of the UCL operation is centered largely within the high school crowd; even so, a surprisingly large number of Claremont State students find the atmosphere and diversions of the game room pleasantly relaxing.

The third area within UCL is situated to the right of the central dining space and serves as a television viewing lounge. The room is spacious, easily holding the 10 tables (seating 40 people) that are placed there. Until today, a second hand, 21-inch (diagonally measured) color television set was utilized as an entertainment vehicle in the lounge. The set was placed on a viewing stand built into the wall above the small bar in the room. The bar houses the hardware needed to serve beer and soft drinks in the TV lounge. Fifteen bar stools rim the edge of the bar and are considered the choice viewing areas for the major sporting events that are always tuned in by Richard James. Next to the fundamental operation of the business, James enjoys a good ball game on his color set more than just about anything.

This afternoon, the 8-year old set failed to operate properly, for the third time in as many weeks. The disgruntled owner of UCL decided to replace the erratic set before he lost too many of his regular TV lounge patrons. Anyway, prior to this problem, James had been dissatisfied with the volume of business in the lounge area. He knew that an additional 6 tables and 24 chairs could be placed comfortably in the viewing room, should the level of sales warrant it. So, he retired to his small office to examine some material on available television mechanisms that he had been collecting for the last 6 months.

Rather quickly, James was able to narrow his choice of possible investments to two mutually exclusive entertainment systems. He definitely would purchase either (1) a conventional color set with a 25-inch (diagonaly measured) screen, or (2) a product called Video-Projector, which offers a 24-square foot (6 feet high by 4 feet wide) viewing area along with an extremely clear image. The Video-Projector is several times more costly than the conventional set, so James found analysis of this potential acquisition to be anything but easy. He immediately called Daniel Ruggins, the Certified Public Accountant who handles all of James' tax matters and also serves as his financial advisor. Ruggins has dealt with UCL during the entire five years that it has been open and is quite familiar with the firm's revenue and cost structure. Upon arriving at UCL, Ruggins met with James and began to develop the data necessary for making an effective choice between the two television systems.

First, they discussed the investment outlay required for each project. The conventional set costs $700 delivered and installed. James thought that the higher level of sales coming from this asset purchase could be achieved only if added inventory in the form of more food, drink, and utensils were kept on hand. The value of this inventory buildup was put at $200.

The Video-Projector could be purchased for $3,800, including setup costs. James decided that to maximize sales revenue during peak hours in the lounge area, this alternative would entail more seating capacity. He would add 6 tables at a unit cost of $30 and 24 chairs at a unit cost of $10. The additional inventory associated with this asset choice was valued at $300. Both Ruggins and James agreed that the inventory buildup for either project would be considered a permanent addition to the asset structure of the firm. This meant that the funds tied up by the inventory rise would not be freed when the television project expired; rather, some other vehicle for maintaining the higher sales level would be found.

The assets of UCL were always depreciated using the straight line method. A five-year time horizon was decided upon as the relevant period for the analysis. This was because James envisioned by that time he would either be ready to construct his own building, allowing him to operate a more sophisticated type of eating establishment, or he would completely remodel his leased facilities and accomplish the same purpose. This longer run business and career objective meant that the bulk of UCL's assets would be sold five years from now. Because of rather rough treatment in the lounge, the salvage value on both sets was placed at zero. Likewise, no scrap value was placed on the tables and chairs that would be purchased as part of the Video-Projector alternative.

At this point, James and Ruggins directed their attention toward development of the expected benefits from each of the prospective investments. The seating capacities for each room of the operation were summarized for review. These figures are contained in Exhibit 1. Upon review of this data, James and Ruggins felt totally comfortable with the estimates of no new seats being needed for the conventional set alternative and 24 being necessary to exploit fully the novelty aspect of the Video-Projector. While at most times the restaurant appeared to be 70 percent full, an average day's business would draw about 218 customers into the UCL. The relationship of customers to total seats was referred to as the "current seating factor" (CSF) by Ruggins. He had observed that the CSF of 1.5 times was rather stable over the years for this company. Because of this stability, he readily used the CSF as a forecasting statistic. Even if the TV lounge area was replaced with ordinary dining space, James felt certain that the CSF of 1.5 could be maintained. The benefits of the imminent purchase, then, would be projected above this base level of business activity.

EXHIBIT 1

University City Lounge
Room Seating Capacities

	Main Dining Area	Game Room	TV Lounge
Current Seats	70	20	55
Average Number of Excess Seats	14	4	25
Additional Seats Needed for Conventional Set Project	0	0	0
Additional Seats Needed for Video-Projector Project	0	0	24

Total Current Capacity: 145 seats

Total Capacity with Video-Projector Project: 169 seats

Noting that the students of Claremont State often complained of the bland flavoring of institutional food, James operated UCL on all 365 days of the year. As a popular, alternative dining establishment, it was profitable for UCL to maintain such extended hours. Sunday often turned out to be a high volume day, due largely to the telecasting of pro football games and also to the fact that an Allegheny County ordinance permitted beer sales on any day of the week.

To place the derivation of revenue estimates into an orderly perspective, Ruggins directed James' attention to Exhibits 2 and 3.

EXHIBIT 2

University City Lounge
Condensed Income Statement for Last Year

	$	%
Net sales	$358,000	100.0%
Cost of goods sold	187,592	52.4
Gross profit	$170,408	47.6%
Other expenses	136,040	38.0
Profit before taxes	$ 34,368	9.6%
Taxes	9,997	2.8
Net profit	$ 24,371	6.8%

EXHIBIT 3

University City Lounge
Sales Analysis by Customer

A. (Current seating factor) X (Current capacity) = Normal number of
customers per day

   (1.5)   X   (145)   = 218

B. (Annual sales)/(Annual operating days)   = Normal sales per day
   (358,000) /(365)   = $981 per day

C. (Normal sales per day) / (Number of customers per day) = Average sales
per customer

   (981)   /   (218)   = $4.50

Last year, UCL earned $24,371 after taxes. The "other expenses" line item shown in the Condensed Income Statement includes a $14,000 annual salary (drawn on a biweekly basis) earned by James as the operating manager. The cost of goods sold, which amounted to 52.4 percent of the $358,000 in net sales, is primarily a variable expense. The other expenses (38 percent of last year's sales) are mainly fixed. Ruggins stated that he thought the use of 52 percent would accurately reflect the cash operating costs occasioned by any sales increases brought on by the television system project. Depreciation charges would be computed separately from this 52 percent of sales factor.

The average tax rate experienced last year by UCL was 29.1 percent. James felt that application of a 29 percent rate for the five-year projection needed in this analysis was reasonable. Ruggins differed, explaining that the adequate growth in income achieved by UCL in the past should continue as long as the local university expanded. This rising income would raise UCL's average tax rate. The C.P.A. suggested using a 34 percent tax rate for the capital expenditure analysis.

James told Ruggins that he hoped the purchase of the conventional set would bring in one additional customer every day of the year. Ruggins called that estimate overly optimistic and proceeded to demonstrate that assertion to his client. He drew upon the calculations contained in Exhibit 3, which show that a typical customer spends $4.50 on each visit to UCL.

One net new customer every operating day translates into an annual sales gain of $1,643. Ruggins told James that as a roundhouse guess (without actually working through the figures), he felt the incremental cash flows from that large a sales increase would result in an internal rate of return of about 75 percent.

"No new ordinary set will give you that high a return, Rick."

"I'm convinced," James replied.

After a few more intense hours of questions and concentration, the two

EXHIBIT 4

University City Lounge
Projected Sales Increase From
One Additional Customer per Day

A.   (New customers per day) X (Annual operating days)   = Equivalent new
                                                            annual
                                                            customers

          (1)   X   (365)   = 365

B.   (Equivalent new annual customers)   X (Average sales = Projected
                                            per customer)   sales increase

               (365)   X   (4.50)   = $1,643

men arrived at some projections in which they had confidence. In Exhibit 5, information relates to the conventional set option. At the most, James could now foresee a net increase of six-tenths of a new customer per day during each year of the project's useful life; that possibility was given only a 10 percent chance of occurring.

EXHIBIT 5

University City Lounge
Projected New Customers per Day
Conventional Set Project

New Customers per Day[1]	Probability of Occurrence[1]
.15	.10
.20	.20
.33	.40
.40	.20
.60	.10

[1] Assumed to be the same for each year of the investment horizon.

The estimates dealing with the Video-Projector differ materially from the conventional set projections. A 24-square foot viewing screen has proven to be an extraordinarily popular attraction in eating establishments located in other university-dominated locales. The device projects the red, green, and blue colors forming the image onto the curved screen from a control panel located 12 feet from it. Advertisements claimed that the picture is so precise the viewer can see the "grain on the bat" or the "laces on the ball." James strongly felt that these distinguishing features of the Video-Projector would attract large crowds to the TV lounge for sporting events and better-than-average movies. More optimism, then, characterized the forecast tied to this option. Ruggins cautioned that any other restaurant in town also could buy the same device. Exhibit 6 tabulates their final assessment related to this possible purchase.

EXHIBIT 6

University City Lounge
Projected New Customers per Day
Video-Projector Project

Years 1-2	New Customers per Day	Probability of Occurrence
	1.00	.20
	2.00	.60
	3.80	.20
Years 3-5	.85	.30
	1.70	.40
	3.20	.30

With this work accomplished, Ruggins returned to his office to begin a detailed analysis of the mutually exclusive investment opportunities. Before leaving, he and James had arrived at a consensus on two other points. First, James could invest in essentially risk-free treasury securities of comparable maturity to the life of the television project and earn an after-tax return of 5 percent. Second, during the investment horizon, the average sales per customer level of $4.50 would be assumed to remain constant.

QUESTIONS

1. Compute the expected net present value and profitability index for each project.

2. Compute the standard deviation about the expected net present value for each project.

3. Compute and graph the cumulative distribution of the profitability index for each project. Use the following cumulative probabilities:

    .10
    .20
    .30
    .40
    .50
    .60
    .70
    .80
    .90
    .95

4. Which system do you recommend that James purchase?

Section 4

The Cost
of
Capital

Case 1

MALLORY ELECTRIC CORPORATION

(Part I: Cost of Capital)

The Mallory Electric Corporation manufactures electric motors used in air conditioning and heating systems. The motors range in size from fractional horsepower models up to the UP-37, which generates 30 plus horsepower. Mallory produces motors for both Currier and Whorlpool, as well as several smaller manufacturers for use in both commercial and residential systems.

During the past 10 years the firm's growth has been very rapid. Mallory grew from a small regional manufacturing firm with annual sales of less than $8,000,000 in 1964 to a major supplier of electric motors with annual sales of over $24,000,000 in 1973. The firm's growth can be largely attributed to two factors—the aggressive efforts of its president, David Wort, and the building boom that continued throughout most of the past 10 years.

Wort has become increasingly apprehensive about the rapidity with which the firm has been expanding (from total assets of roughly $8,000,000 in 1964 to over $18,000,000 in 1973). The expansion has resulted in increasing dependence of the firm on external sources of financing. The firm has had to sell stock and bonds amounting to over $6,000,000 in the last eight years to supplement retained earnings in financing its rapidly expanding needs for funds. Wort's principal concern is that the firm's method for evaluating capital investment proposals may allow it to accept unprofitable projects. The firm had, in the past, simply compared the expected rate of return of a proposed investment with the estimated cost of the specific source of funds used to finance the assets acquisition. However, in those instances where new common stock was sold or internally generated funds were used, the firm arbitrarily used a 15 percent required rate of return. This figure was one that Wort felt would be "adequate," but which he had no sound basis for using.

Wort voiced his concern over the present capital budgeting procedure before the monthly meeting of the heads of each of the operating divisions of the company. Among those present was John Howard, the recently appointed chief financial officer. Howard had also considered the problem of determining the cutoff rate for new capital investments and had even attempted to estimate the firm's cost of capital. However, he had encountered a number of difficulties. Among them were the following:

1. He did not know which sources of financing should be incorporated into his calculations. Specifically, there was the problem of whether to include certain sources of short-term funds such as accounts payable and accrued or deferred expense items, in the cost of capital computation. Howard felt that since these short-term funds were not used to finance the purchase of fixed or permanent assets (included in the firm's capital budget), they probably should be omitted from consideration in determining the estimate of the cost of capital.

2. Howard felt that the cost of all relevant sources of financing should be made a part of the cost of capital, but he was uncertain as to whether book or market value weights or possibly some alternative weighting system should be used to measure their relative importance. He did know, however, that Wort felt the present capital structure was the best the firm could achieve in terms of both current market conditions and basic business risk exposure.

3. Finally, the cost of equity funds was particularly troublesome. Howard felt that the firm's earnings and dividends would probably continue to grow at an annual rate of 6 to 8 percent, but had been unable to incorporate this estimate into a viable cost of equity capital.

When Howard told Wort of his attempts to estimate the firm's cost of capital, Wort was very interested and asked that he prepare a report concerning the cost of capital for the next year's capital budget consisting of $2,000,000 in planned asset acquisitions (beyond those assets whose purchase could be financed with funds from noncash charges). Most of the new capital budget was related to a planned expansion in the firm's existing plant and facilities.

QUESTIONS

1. What set of weights should be used in estimating a firm's cost of capital? Correspondingly, what sources of funds should be made a part of the cost of capital estimate?

2. Using the information in Exhibits 1 and 2, estimate the firm's marginal

EXHIBIT 1

In a series of discussions with potential suppliers of funds, Mallory had obtained the following information:

A. New bonds similar to those now outstanding can be sold to net the company $950 per bond with a 9.5 percent coupon and 25-year maturity. The bonds would be callable only after five-years and at a price of 108.5 for the sixth year with the call premium declining linearly over a 20-year period.

B. Preferred stock with a 9 percent dividend and a $100 per value could be sold to net the company $100 per share after issue expenses.

C. Mallory's common stock is actively traded over-the-counter and is presently selling for around $50 a share. Issue costs on new common are roughly $5 per share, and the firm would probably have to lower the stock price by another $5 to facilitate the sale.

D. Funds available to help finance the planned expansion from next year's earnings are expected to equal $400,000. Also, dividends per share on common stock for 1974 are expected to be $4.

EXHIBIT 2

Mallory Electric Corporation

Balance Sheet
for the Year Ended 12/31/73

Assets	Liabilities and Capital	
	Accounts payable	$ 500,000
	Accrued expenses	250,000
	Notes payable	1,250,000[1]
	Current liabilities	2,000,000
	First mortage bonds	
	(5-3/4% due in 1988)	4,000,000
	Preferred stock (6% with $100 par)	2,000,000
	Common stock ($10 par)	1,000,000
	Paid-in capital[2]	2,000,000
	Retained earnings	7,000,000
$18,000,000		$18,000,000

[1]Payable in monthly installments over the next two years including interest of 7 percent per annum.

[2]Paid-in capital resulted from the sale of both preferred and common stock in the following amounts:

	Paid-in Capital
Preferred stock	$1,000,000
Common stock	1,000,000

cost of capital for the planned expansion. You may use a 50 percent marginal income tax rate in your calculations.

3. Would the cutoff rate have been different had the expansion been $6,000,000 instead of $2,000,000? What would have been the cost of the added $4,000,000?

4. If the firm decided to use only long-term debt to supplement retained earnings in financing the capital expenditures, how would this affect the cost of capital? (No computations required — discuss briefly.)

5. If the planned capital expenditures should involve a change in the basic riskiness of the firm, how would this affect the usefulness of the computed cost of capital? Discuss briefly.

Case 1

MALLORY ELECTRIC CORPORATION

(Part II: Cost of Capital)

John Howard, chief financial officer for Mallory Electric, has recently been assigned responsibility for estimating the cost of capital for his firm. Much of the work has been routine, such as generating cost estimates for borrowed funds and preferred stock; however, Howard encountered some very troublesome problems when attempting to cost new equity and retained earnings. The principal difficulty arose in conjunction with the very erratic pattern of dividend growth the firm has experienced in the past, which simply does not fit the requirements of the valuation model Howard was trying to use in estimating the cost of equity. Specifically, the valuation model he was attempting to use made the explicit assumption that the stock being valued must be expected to experience a constant rate of growth in common dividends into the indefinite future. In light of the firm's past dividend payment record, and what Howard believed the future pattern of dividend payments to be, this assumption was simply untenable.

While reading through a well known journal devoted to the problems of financial management, Howard ran across an article that described how to use the capital asset pricing model to estimate the cost of equity capital.[1] The

[1]J. Fred Weston, "Investment Decisions Using the Capital Asset Pricing Model," *Financial Management* (Spring 1973), pp. 25-33.

suggested approach was particularly appealing to Howard in that it did not require that any unrealistic assumption be made regarding the pattern of future growth in common dividends. Also, the technique appeared, at least on the surface, to be relatively simple to apply.

From the article, Howard found that there were three basic steps involved in using the capital asset pricing model in connection with the estimation of the cost of equity. First, he would have to estimate the riskiness of the firm in terms of its systematic or nondiversifiable risk (referred to in the article as the beta coefficient). This first step required that historical return information be gathered for the firm's common stock, the market as a whole, and for the riskless asset. This data has been compiled and is presented in Exhibit 1. The second step in the procedure involved estimating expected annual returns for the market for all stocks and for the riskless asset. The third and final step then involved simply substituting the appropriate estimates into the capital asset pricing model. The procedure certainly appeared simple enough, so Howard decided to adopt it as one estimate of the firm's cost of equity capital.

EXHIBIT 1

Annual Return Data For Mallory Electric, the Market and the Risk Free Rate of Interest

Year	Market Returns	Risk Free Rate of Interest	Stock Returns for Mallory
0	.08	.03	.10
1	.12	.04	.11
2	.10	.04	.08
3	.23	.05	.28
4	(.08)	.06	(.12)
5	.16	.05	.15
6	.14	.05	.12
7	.12	.07	.08
8	(.04)	.06	(.08)
9	.18	.07	.22

QUESTIONS

1. Using the information in Exhibit 1, compute Mallory's beta coefficient. Is Mallory's stock more or less risky than the market portfolio? Explain.

2. What is the required return on equity capital for Mallory in accordance with the capital asset pricing model?

3. What practical and theoretical problems do you see that Mallory and other firms might encounter in attempting to use the capital asset pricing model to estimate the cost of equity capital?

Case 2

WESTERN ENERGY DEVELOPMENT, INCORPORATED

(Cost of Capital)

In May of 1976, Linda Bellich, a recent MBA graduate and newly appointed assistant to the comptroller of Western Energy Development, Incorporated (WED), was given a list of six new investment projects proposed for the following year. It was her job to analyze these projects and be prepared to present her findings before the board of directors at their annual meeting to be held in 10 days.

Western Energy Development was founded in Laramie, Wyoming, in 1948 by Scott Heywood. WED gained recognition as a leading producer of high quality coal, with the majority of its sales being made to Japan. During the post-World War II era, with the rapid economic expansion of Japan, demand not only for coal but for other energy products boomed, and WED's sales grew rapidly. As a result of this rapid growth and recognition of new opportunities in the energy market, WED began to diversify its product line. While retaining its emphasis on coal production, it expanded operations to include uranium mining, the production of electrical generators, and finally made its way into all phases of energy production. By 1975, WED's sales had reached the $140 million level, with net profit after tax reaching a record $6.7 million.

As WED expanded its product line in the late 1960s, it also formalized its capital budgeting procedure. Until 1967, capital investment projects were selected primarily as a result of the average return on investment calculations, with individual departments submitting these calculations for projects falling within its division. In 1971 this procedure was replaced by one using present value as the decision-making criteria. This change was made to incorporate cash flows rather than accounting profits into the decision-making analysis in addition to adjusting these flows for the time value of money. At that time the cost of capital for WED was determined to be 4.36 percent, which has been used as the discount rate for the past 5 years. This rate was determined by taking a weighted average of the costs WED had incurred in raising funds from the capital markets over the previous 10 years.

It had originally been Bellich's assignment to update this rate over the most recent 10-year period and determine the net present value of all of the proposed investment opportunities using this newly calculated figure. However, she objected to this procedure, stating that while this calculation gave a good estimate of "the past cost" of capital, changing interest rates and stock prices made this calculation of little value. Bellich suggested that current costs of raising funds in the capital markets be weighted by their percentage makeup of the capital structure. This proposal was reviewed enthusiastically by the comptroller of WED, and Bellich was given the assignment of recalculating WED's cost of capital and providing a written report for the financial board of directors explaining and justifying this calculation.

To determine a weighted average cost of capital for WED, it was necessary for Linda Bellich to examine the costs associated with each source of funding used. In the past, the largest sources of funding had been through the issuance of new common stock and internally generated funds. Through conversations with the comptroller and other members of the board of directors, Bellich learned that the firm, in fact, wishes to maintain its current financial structure (shown in Exhibit 1). She further determined that the strong growth patterns that WED had exhibited over the past 10 years were expected to continue indefinitely. This was due to the dwindling supply of U.S. and Japanese domestic oil and the growing importance of, and U.S. and Japanese dependence upon, coal and other alternative energy resources. Through further investigation, Bellich learned that WED could issue additional shares of common stock, which had a par value of $25 per share and were selling at a current market price of $45. The expected dividend for the next period would be $2 per share, with expected growth at a rate of 6 percent per year for the forseeable future. The underwriting commission paid to WED's investment banker would amount to $2 per share and would be for insuring the issue against the risk of adverse market fluctuations in the stock's selling price during the distribution process, in addition to performing the function of actually selling the security and providing advice as to the timing and pricing of the issue.

Preferred stock at 6 percent also could be issued with the help of an investment banker at $97 per share with a par value of $100 per share. Of this $97,

EXHIBIT 1

Western Energy Development, Incorporated

Balance Sheet
for Year ending April 30, 1976

Assets

Cash	$ 9,000,000
Accounts Receivable	31,000,000
Inventories	12,000,000
Total Current Assets	52,000,000
Net Fixed Assets	193,000,000
Goodwill	7,000,000
Total Assets	$252,000,000

Liabilities & Equity

Accounts Payable	$ 850,000
Current Debt	10,000,000
Accrued Taxes	1,150,000
Total Current Liabilities	12,000,000
Long-Term Debt	72,000,000
Preferred Stock	43,000,000
Common Stock	114,000,000
Retained Earnings	11,000,000
Total Liabilities & Equity	$252,000,000

3.1 percent would go to the investment banker for his help in marketing the issue, with the remainder of the funds going to WED.

Finally, Bellich learned that it would be possible for WED to raise an additional $1 million through a one-year loan from WED's Chicago bank at 9 percent. Any amount raised over $1 million would cost WED 14 percent. Short-term debt always has been used by Western to finance capital expenditures, and as WED grows it is expected to maintain its proportion in the capital structure to support capital expansion. Also, $6 million could be raised through a bond issue with 30 years maturity with a 10 percent coupon at 98 percent of face value. On this issue, 2 percent of the face value would be charged as an underwriting commission. If it became necessary to raise more funds via long-term debt, $3 million more could be accumulated, with the additional 30 year bonds being sold at 95 percent of face value with the coupon rate being raised to 11 percent and 2 percent of the value being charged as an underwriting commission. While any additional funds raised via long-term debt would necessarily have a 30-year maturity with a 14 percent coupon yield and be sold at 95 percent of face value, 2 percent of this face value would be charged as an underwriting fee. Here again, this fee would go to the investment banker for his help in marketing the issue.

In the past, WED has calculated a weighted average of these sources of

funds to determine its cost of capital. In discussions with the current comptroller, the point was raised that while this served as an appropriate calculation
for externally generated funds, it did not take into account the fact that much
of the funds used for capital expenditures by WED were internally generated.
For example, WED is expected to produce $5 million in depreciation generated
funds in addition to retaining $4 million of its earnings during the coming
period. The comptroller agreed that there should be some cost associated with
retained earning financing incorporated into the calculations, but depreciation
charges should not be included since they, as opposed to all other financing
methods, do not appear on the liability side of the balance sheet. Although Bellich
was not completely convinced by the comptroller's logic, she continued with
her work.

QUESTIONS

1. Should Linda Bellich assign a cost to any depreciation generated funds?
    If so, what should be the cost assigned? Should this cost be used in the
    calculations of the average cost of capital? If not, what is its significance?

2. Should Bellich assign a cost to funds from retained earnings? Why or why
    not? If so, what cost should be assigned? (Assume no personal taxes or
    brokerage fees.) Would this cost change if the stockholder pays an income
    tax on dividends in addition to incurring brokerage costs when reinvesting
    dividend receipts?

3. Assuming WED wishes to continue with the existing capital structure,
    what is the average cost of capital associated with the next $25 million
    increase in net assets? (Use a 50 percent corporate tax rate for WED.)

4. Graph WED's marginal cost of capital associated with the first $40 million
    generated, again assuming WED desires to maintain its current capital
    structure. Observing this supply curve of capital, do you now feel it is
    possible to determine the cost of capital independently of the amount
    of funds to be raised?

5. At the board of directors meeting, the projected costs and internal rates
    of return for the six capital investment projects is given as follows:

Project	Cost	IRR
1	$7M	8.73%
2	$7M	8.40%
3	$8M	9.60%
4	$5M	9.14%
5	$5M	8.20%
6	$8M	8.18%

    Graph the internal rates of return on investment projects against the
    marginal cost of capital. Which projects should be selected?

6. If dividends are expected to be as given below, and the net proceeds to the company from the sale of a share of stock are $43.25, what is Ke?

$$D_1 = 1.00$$
$$D_2 = 2.00$$
$$D_3 = 3.00$$
$$D_4 = 4.00$$
$$D_5 \text{ through } D_\infty = 6.00$$

7. If the projects being selected by WED have a higher degree of risk than do current projects, what will happen to the cost of capital over time? If projects being selected have less risk than do current projects, what will happen to the cost of capital over time?

8. How might a change in the long-term interest rate (a change upward or a change downward) affect the marginal cost of equity capital and the overall marginal cost of capital?

Case 3

TEXON PRODUCTION, INC.

(Cost of Capital)

In 1912, Imir Swenson, a Swedish immigrant, migrated to the south plains of Texas to begin cotton farming. His farming operation continued to expand, with the only downturn coming during the depression in the 1930s. After the depression, his operation resumed a growth posture; however, in 1940, he made a decision to retire. At this time his two sons, only nearing their twenties, assumed control of the farming interests and proved not only to be excellent farmers but equally capable businessmen. However, during World War II, the two young men temporarily set aside their farming activities to enlist in the army. Upon their return home in 1945, they resumed their partnership. The business scope remained virtually unchanged until Joseph Swenson convinced his brother Herman that the processing of raw cotton would represent a profitable expansion of business interests. With the financial support of their father, the necessary plant and equipment was acquired. This additional capability became operational in October 1947.

During the ensuing years, the mixture of the firm's revenues gradually shifted from farm production to cotton processing. As this change in business purpose became more extensive, the existing partnership came under pressure for additional capital. As the Swensons approached prospective investors, some hesitancy was encountered as a result of the current form of business, that is, the partnership. The private parties being contacted were simply not interested in subjecting themselves to the unlimited liability associated with a partnership. For this reason, in 1965 the business was incorporated, with the new corporate entity being designated as Texon Production, Inc.

At the time of incorporation, Joseph Swenson became president of the business, with the complete emphasis of the firm being placed upon the processing of cotton. During his presidency, the company has continued to prosper, with both sales and earnings growing at a relatively stable rate. (The company's financial condition for the past five years is reflected in Exhibit 1.) Earnings before interest and taxes have been running at approximately 25 percent of net sales, with an increase to about 30 percent by 1980 being expected. (The projected sales levels for the next five years are shown in Exhibit 2.) The reason for the projected improvement in the profitability margins comes from improved processing equipment and favorable market conditions.

Since the inception of the corporation, capital assets have expanded at a rate approximating 10 percent per year. Exhibit 3 provides an indication of the growth pattern in capital expenditures within the past five years. Capital needs for 1978 are expected to be significantly larger than experienced in prior years, with an estimate having been set at $275,000. These funds are to be used in renovating the plant and to purchase new processing and distribution equipment. Joseph Swenson is particularly interested in a new process that would allow for more efficient cleaning of the cotton fiber. Although the 1978 projection for capital needs is substantially higher than in previous periods, the management policy of appropriating a portion of retained earnings for investments has not been altered to account for the forthcoming investment level.

As to the corporation's financial policies, management has maintained a relatively constant capital structure and dividend pay-out ratio. The firm's capital structure is considered by Joseph Swenson to be optimal and at a level that should be maintained for the foreseeable future. He maintains this conviction in spite of the fact that the percentage of debt financing for the industry, currently at 15 percent, is considerably lower than the same figure for Texon Production. In contrast, Herman Swenson is somewhat concerned regarding the capital-mix decision. The basis for his anxiety rests upon several factors, including the firm's poor liquidity position. Next, he contends that if the current financial policy is not changed, any future notes payable, regardless of maturity structure, would have a cost of 11 percent. Furthermore, the existing bonds, which consist of 252 securities have a $1,000 par value, are currently depressed at a market value of $855. Finally, the preferred stock has encountered a decrease in market price to $88. For these reasons, he has asked Joseph Swenson to reconsider his position regarding the concern's financial mix. As to the dividend policy, the company paid out 31.34 percent of its earnings in 1977. This relationship has been maintained relatively closely in the past and is expected to continue into the indefinite future.

EXHIBIT 1

Texon Production, Inc.

Comparative Balance Sheet

Assets	1973	1974
Cash	$ 16,811	$ 18,430
Marketable securities	125,874	136,216
Receivables	45,617	42,210
Inventory	178,343	184,355
Property, plant and equipment (net)	616,634	653,212
	$983,279	$1,034,423

Liabilities and Stockholders' Equity		
Trade payables	$ 16,593	$ 18,219
Short-term notes (6%, due 12/31/78)	17,359	16,230
Notes payable (8%, 15 yrs., due 1/1/88)	30,882	30,882
Bonds payable (8%, 20 yrs., due 1/1/88)	252,000	252,000
Preferred stock ($9 cumulative $100 par, 2,000 shares authorized, 1,000 shares issued)	100,000	100,000
Common stock ($10 par, 50,000 shares authorized)	254,310	254,830
Paid-in-capital in excess of par:		
Preferred	2,000	2,000
Common	34,198	50,103
Retained earnings:		
Appropriated	55,325	63,280
Free	220,612	246,879
	$983,279	$1,034,423

EXHIBIT 1 (Continued)

Texon Production, Inc.

Comparative Balance Sheet

1975	1976	1977
$ 21,203	$ 19,821	$ 20,611
148,821	153,260	176,215
62,533	78,330	89,800
211,216	203,820	224,074
717,240	784,215	816,107
$1,161,013	$1,239,446	$1,326,807
$ 23,416	$ 21,210	$ 22,311
21,870	23,210	25,637
30,882	30,882	30,882
252,000	252,000	252,000
100,000	100,000	100,000
255,100	253,870	254,900
2,000	2,000	2,000
128,557	169,182	209,175
68,412	77,526	176,215
278,776	309,566	253,687
$1,161,013	$1,239,446	$1,326,807

EXHIBIT 1 (Continued)

Texon Production, Inc.

Comparative Income Statement

	1973	1974	1975	1976	1977
Net sales	$449,206	$447,683	$508,133	$539,571	$576,424
Cost of goods sold	255,980	243,012	289,642	307,558	332,341
Operating expenses	80,913	86,003	91,472	97,125	100,998
Earnings before interest and taxes	$112,313	$118,668	$127,019	$134,888	$143,085
Interest	23,672	23,604	23,942	24,023	24,168
Taxable earnings	$ 88,641	$ 95,064	$103,077	$110,865	$118,917
Income taxes	35,307	38,026	41,362	44,359	47,567
Earning after taxes	$ 53,334	$ 57,038	$ 61,715	$ 66,506	$ 71,350
Preferred dividend	9,000	9,000	9,000	9,000	9,000
Net income	$ 44,334	$ 48,038	$ 52,715	$ 57,506	$ 62,350
Earnings per share	$ 1.74	1.89	2.07	2.27	2.45
Dividends per share	.52	.55	.62	.70	.77

As a new financial policy, Herman Swenson has decided to calculate the firm's cost of capital. He knows very little about the actual computations and associated assumptions, and has approached the treasurer Bernard Erickson for

EXHIBIT 2

Projected Sales

1978	$600,000
1979	625,000
1980	668,000
1981	705,000
1982	783,000

assistance. In response, Erickson has begun a search for additional information that would be needed in making the cost-of-capital determination. In this effort,

EXHIBIT 3

Capital Outlay

1973	$56,774
1974	62,933
1975	93,089
1976	76,452
1977	83,178

he has come to the conclusion that an issuance of any additional common stock or preferred stock would have a flotation cost of some 10 percent. Any future bond issues would face an 8 percent issuance cost. Furthermore, the current risk-free rate, as reflected by short-term government securities, is 5 percent. Finally, a "beta factor" for Texon Production, Inc., using the last 10 years of annual data, has been ascertained to be 1.32. In this regard, the average annual returns of the market have been computed, with the results indicated in Exhibit 5.

EXHIBIT 4

Market Price of Common Stock for 1977

Jan. 31	$14.00
Feb. 28	14.50
March 31	15.25
April 30	14.95
May 31	15.85
June 30	16.60
July 31	17.50
Aug. 31	18.25
Sept. 30	17.90
Oct. 31	18.75
Nov. 30	19.10
Dec. 31	19.50

QUESTIONS

1. When management computes its firm's cost of capital, what application(s) might be made of the measurement?

2. What assumptions are attached to the calculations?

3. Using the existing capital structure, expressed in terms of market value as opposed to book value, determine the firm's weighted cost of capital as of January 1, 1978, at the projected 1978 investment level. Assume (1) the existing capital committed to marketable securities is a viable source of internal funds; (2) the book values for credit and all notes closely reflect

EXHIBIT 5

Average Annual Return for the Market

1977	.23
1976	.17
1975	(.08)
1974	.02
1973	.13
1972	.09
1971	(.01)
1970	.16
1969	.21
1968	.07

the current market value of such forms of indebtedness; (3) no implicit costs exist for trade credit and all trade discounts are taken; and (4) a company tax rate of 40 percent.

4. How well do you consider the assumptions cited in question 2 to have been met?

5. Drawing upon the capital asset-pricing model to determine the company's cost of equity, recompute the weighted cost of capital for Texon Production, Inc.

Section 5

Long-Term Financing Decisions

Case 1

SPECIALTY AUTO PARTS

(Financial Leverage Analysis)

Specialty Auto Parts (SAP) is located in Toledo, Ohio. The firm was founded in 1919 by C. K. Blackburn, who served as president and chairman of the board until his death in early 1976. Both positions are now filled by Ken Blackburn, C. K.'s eldest son, who is carrying on his father's dogmatic tradition of "high quality products for a quality industry." Mark Dennis, vice-president of finance, often argued formally and informally against the total emphasis contained in the latter four words of that phrase, which trademarked all of SAP's advertisements. Dennis simply felt that by concentrating upon supplying component parts only to the auto industry, an undue exposure to basic business risk was assumed.

SAP manufactures a very wide range of component parts, subassemblies, and final assemblies for sale to the major automobile producers, who are largely concentrated 61 miles north, in Detroit. Standard items in the product line include hubs, rims, brakes, antiskid units, and mirrors. C. K. Blackburn had taken immense pride in all facets of SAP's activities, ranging from the early decision to locate in Toledo to the firm's solid reputation within key offices in Detroit's Fisher Building. In retrospect, the location decision was a fine one. An expressway connects Toledo with Detroit, making truck transportation extremely swift. Further, Toledo is located on the west end of Lake Erie, with a good port facility, enabling the firm to receive raw materials via marine transportation and to ship finished goods to other key automotive centers, such as Cleveland across the lake.

Blackburn family interests own 51 percent of the common stock of SAP. Over the years outside financing has been almost completely shunned by the organization. The SAP annual report of four years past contains this statement: "We will continue to finance corporate growth primarily through the internal generation of funds." Recent auto industry trends, however, have necessitated a shift by SAP management away from strict adherence to that policy. A national recession saw last year's motor vehicle factory sales of passenger cars drop 24 percent from the previous annual period. This, in turn, adversely affected the profitability and funds-generating capacity of SAP. On top of this, the officials of SAP have decided upon a major product mix shift. The firm underestimated the demand for disc brakes, which have been installed on about 84 to 86 percent of passenger cars in recent years (see Exhibit 1). SAP's capacity to produce in this area will be increased during the next year. The volume achieved on the sale of antiskid units has proved to be a disappointment. Accordingly, some factory space and equipment devoted to this product line will be redeployed into other more profitable activities.

Noting the public's acceptance of rear window defoggers, the firm has developed the technology necessary to be competitive in this product. To effect this expertise, however, substantial equipment purchases will be required within the next six months. The end result is that SAP must raise $6 million in the capital markets through either the sale of new common stock or the issuance of bonds. The new common shares could be sold to net the firm $48 per share. The common stock price of SAP shares in the marketplace is now $54. Allen Winthrop, who is a partner in the investment banking house long used by SAP, has assured Mark Dennis that the new bond issue could be placed with an 8 percent interest rate. Winthrop's counsel always has been highly valued by Dennis and other members of the SAP top management team.

EXHIBIT 1

Specialty Auto Parts

Factory Installations of Selected Equipment
(Percent of Total Units Installed Upon)

Automobile Equipment	Most Recent Year	One Year Earlier
Power brakes, 4-wheel drum	2.4	1.0
Power brakes, 2 or 4-wheel disc	64.8	74.5
Disc brakes manual	19.2	11.2
Skid control device	0.9	1.9
Rear window defogger	21.5	16.4

Source: *1975 Automobile Facts & Figures,* Motor Vehicle Manufacturers Association, 1975, p. 21.

A preliminary meeting took place one week ago with Dennis, Winthrop, and Ken Blackburn in attendance. The only topic discussed was the $6 million financing choice facing SAP. Exhibits 2, 3, and 4 were analyzed at length. Dennis felt that the firm's owners would benefit if the asset expansion were financed with debt capital. Also, Blackburn liked having total control over the firm's operations. With 51 percent of the common shares family owned, Blackburn knew that he could personally choose a course of action when a tough situation faced SAP. Incidentally, the corporate charter of SAP does not provide for the election of directors via a cumulative voting procedure.

EXHIBIT 2

Specialty Auto Parts

Abbreviated Balance Sheet, December 31, Last Year

Assets	
Current assets	$14,750,000
Net plant and equipment	19,000,000
Other	2,250,000
Total assets	$36,000,000

Liabilities and Equity	
Current liabilities	$ 4,920,000
Long-term debt:	
First mortgage bonds, 20 years to maturity, at 7%	2,950,000
Common stock, $5 par	5,000,000
Capital surplus	10,000,000
Retained earnings	13,130,000
Total liabilities and equity	$36,000,000

Dennis pointed out to Blackburn that apart from the family, no "public" investor controlled as much as 5 percent of the outstanding common shares. Thus, Dennis noted effective control of the firm's operations would remain with the Blackburn family should the new common stock alternative be elected. Dennis did not think it would be prudent to elect the debt alternative *only* because it would insure Blackburn family control over SAP in the strictest sense.

Both Dennis and Blackburn were concerned with the effect of additional financial leverage upon the firm's price/earnings ratio. To deal partially with this question, Winthrop's staff prepared Exhibit 4. Winthrop suggested to Blackburn that his firm prepare for the "worst that could happen." He stated that SAP's price/earnings ratio might remain unchanged from its present level of 9.59 times if the debt alternative were chosen. He did not, however, believe such an

EXHIBIT 3

Specialty Auto Parts

Income Statement, December 31, Last Year

Sales	$112,000,000
Variable costs	88,476,520
Fixed costs (excluding interest)	12,064,980
Interest expense	206,500
Earnings before taxes	$ 11,252,000
Taxes (at 50%)	5,626,000
Net profit	$ 5,626,000

occurrence to be highly likely. Winthrop offered his best guess that SAP's price/earnings ratio will fall to 9.3 times if bonds are sold and will rise to 10 times if the common stock alternative is selected.

EXHIBIT 4

Specialty Auto Parts

Main Competitors' Selected Financial Relationships

Firm	Debt Ratio[1]	Tier[2]	P/E Ratio[3]
Atlas Auto Components	32.7%	7	7.5
Autonite	20.1%	38	9.5
Kalsey-Ways, Ltd.	24.2%	14	9.0
L-G Parts	26.8%	14	9.0
Morgan-Wells, Inc.	19.0%	29	11.0
Simple average	24.6%	20.4	9.2

[1] Total debt divided by total assets.

[2] Times interest earned ratio.

[3] Price to earnings ratio.

Prior to taking the question before the entire board, Ken Blackburn wanted to review a more substantial body of analysis with Dennis and Winthrop. He gave Dennis a week to prepare the information requested below.

QUESTIONS

1. Dennis has projected that the firm's variable cost to sales ratio will be .79 after the $6 million expansion is effected. In addition, fixed costs apart from interest will rise to an annual level of $13 million. Calculate the level of sales that will equate earnings per share regardless of whether the subject $6 million is financed with bonds or common stock.

2. Set up income statements for bond financing and common stock financing using the sales volume determined above, and demonstrate that earnings per share will indeed be the same under the assumed conditions.

3. Use last year's results as the base period. Compute earnings per share under each financing alternative for sales levels equal to (a) 70 percent, (b) 85 percent, (c) 100 percent, (d) 110 percent, and (e) 120 percent of the base period results.

4. Employing the price/earnings ratios suggested by Winthrop, project the common stock prices for each financing choice at the sales levels just analyzed.

5. Again taking Winthrop's "best guess" price/earnings ratios, determine the sales level that will equate market price per share regardless of the financing source chosen.

6. After reviewing recent marketing department forecasts of sales levels, Ken Blackburn concluded, "Rarely will SAP experience revenues below the $120 million mark." If Blackburn is correct, which financing alternative do you recommend?

Case 2

SAN PABLO BOTTLING COMPANY

(Bonds versus Stock)

San Pablo Bottling Company was founded in 1948 and engages in the sale and distribution of canned and bottled soft drinks in the four-county area surrounding the city of San Pablo, California. Since its founding, the company has limited its operations to the soft drink business, with the result that its primary source of growth has come from the growth in population in the area. In recent years the population boom that occurred throughout most of the 1950s and 1960s has subsided, with a slowing effect on SPB's sales. In fact, SPB's sales have stabilized over the last five years with the exception of minor year-to-year fluctuations. This rather disturbing pattern has caused the management of SPB to consider diversification into different product lines as a source of renewed sales growth.

In its efforts to diversify its product offerings, SPB has recently decided to acquire three smaller companies operating in the San Pablo area. These firms engage in the distribution and sale of prepared food and snack items, sold primarily through vending machines. The companies include the Morten Potato Chip Company, Snacks, Inc., and Morgan Food Distributors, Inc. A partial listing of the product offerings of the proposed acquisitions is found in Exhibit 1. SPB's management has high expectations for the three subsidiaries as they feel that their own expertise in managing the distribution of soft drinks through a similar media will combine very well with the established operations of the firms being acquired.

EXHIBIT 1

New Product Offerings

Morten Potato Chip Company

Morten Potato Chips
Morten Salad Spreads
Jolly Jams and Jellies
El Goucho Party Dips

Snacks, Inc.

Chewee Snack Krackers
Romo Fruit Bar
Chocobar
Prepak Sandwiches

Morgan Food Distributors, Inc.

Seams Ice Cream
Ruth Ann Chocolates
Minces Party Snacks
Dreambar Cookies

To finance the acquisitions, San Pablo must raise $8,000,000 in external capital. The firm's board of directors has considered three alternative methods for raising the needed funds. Each of these alternatives is briefly described below:

Method 1.   A new common stock issue, which SPB has been told can be sold to net the firm approximately $6.50 a share.

Method 2.   A mixture of both common stock and bonds. This alternative would involve the sale of a $5,000,000 issue of common stock involving 830,000 new shares. The remaining $3,000,000 would be raised through a private placement of a bond issue with a group of four life insurance companies. The bonds would carry a 9 percent rate of interest and a 10-year maturity with annual principal and interest payments equal to $467,464.47. Also, the insurance companies would specify that the firm maintain a fixed charge coverage ratio of at least 2.5 times and a long-term debt to total capitalization ratio of 40 percent or less.

Method 3.   The third alternative involves the flotation of a $5,000,000 bond issue. The firm estimates that such an issue would carry a 10 1/2 percent rate of interest and would include covenants similar to those imposed by the life insurance companies in the private placement. Also, a 5-year delayed call with a 6th year call premium set at one year's interest and declining linearly until the 15th year of the 20-year maturity of the issue would be anticipated. The remaining $3,000,000 would be raised through the use of a rights offering whereby three new shares of common stock could be purchased at a subscription price of $5 per share for each four shares held. Based on a current price for the firm's common stock of $7.25, the board of directors of SPB feels that the offering has an excellent chance of success.

San Pablo's chief financial officer feels that one of the prime considerations in making the financing decision is the impact of that decision on the earnings available to the firm's owners. In 1975, SPB's operating earnings were slightly down from 1974, but still were over $1 million, which produced a times interest earned ratio of 3.24 (see Exhibit 4 for 1974 and 1975 financial statements). The proposed acquisitions could increase SPB's operating earnings by as much as $1,000,000 per year over and above those earnings attributable to the firm's ongoing operations. From a pessimistic point of view, the newly acquired subsidiaries might increase operating earnings by a modest $500,000, and the firm's management expects the acquisitions will add $800,000 to their operating earnings. Although San Pablo's sales have virtually stabilized in the last few years, they do fluctuate from year to year as is evidenced in the sales figures for the past five years given in Exhibit 2.

EXHIBIT 2

Historical Sales and Earnings

	1975	1974	1973	1972	1971
Sales	$22,703,229	21,418,202	21,404,220	19,788,440	18,280,410
NOI	1,006,820	1,066,065	997,302	978,692	883,774
NI	368,477	406,622	397,721	376,420	352,101
EPS	.46	.51	.50	.47	.44

In surveying the financial practices of a number of firms that are roughly comparable in size to SPB, a set of guidelines or norms has been established. SPB's management feels very strongly that it should not deviate significantly from the practices of similar types of firms with regard to its financial structure policies. The norms or guidelines that SPB feels to be appropriate are found in Exhibit 3.

Frederick K. Willard serves as chairman of SPB's board of directors and is the firm's principal stockholder. Willard owns some 30 percent of the firm's

EXHIBIT 3

Financial Guidelines

Ratio	Norm 1974-1975
Current ratio	1.28X
Acid-test ratio	.87X
Inventory turnover	10.20X
Average collection period	24 days
Long-term debt / total capitalization[1]	40%
Common equity / total assets	43%
Net operating income / interest expense	3.41X
Net operating income / total assets	9.41%
Net income / common equity	8.19%
Net income / total assets	3.52%

[1]Total capitalization = long-term debt + preferred stock + common equity.

common stock and enjoys controlling interest in the firm. Regardless of the decision made, Willard has expressed the strong desire to maintain his controlling interest.

QUESTIONS

1. What factors should be considered in making the financing decision faced by San Pablo Bottling Co.? Discuss each briefly.

2. What is your recommendation to the board of directors of SPB as to the choice they should make? Be sure to consider each of the factors discussed in your answer to question #1 above (within the limits of available information).

EXHIBIT 4

San Pablo Bottling Company

Balance Sheets

Assets

Current	1975	1974
Cash	$ 1,349,524	$ 1,563,424
Accounts receivable	1,438,929	1,628,782
Inventories	1,397,248	1,414,104
Prepaid expenses	348,127	179,213
Total current assets	4,533,828	4,785,523

Property, Plant, and Equipment

	1975	1974
Land	$ 712,614	$ 712,614
Buildings	3,291,400	3,001,264
Machinery, equipment and furniture	2,999,520	2,711,411
Vending machines	5,617,775	4,973,642
Transportation equipment	1,528,291	1,879,122
Total property, plant, and equipment	14,149,600	13,278,053
less accumulated depreciation	7,001,690	6,842,113
Net property, plant, and equipment	7,147,910	6,435,940
Total assets	$11,681,738	$11,221,463

Liabilities and Stockholders Equity

Current	1975	1974
Notes payable (current portion)	$ 1,218,468	$ 1,412,111
Accounts payable	1,624,819	1,794,101
Other liabilities and accrued expenses		
Salaries and wages	51,212	54,188
Accrued taxes	104,031	171,391
Accrued interest	17,811	13,199
Accrued expenses	140,897	167,612
Total current liabilities	3,157,238	3,612,602
Long-term debt (net of current portion)	3,055,639	2,508,477

Stockholders Equity

	1975	1974
Capital stock, authorized 3,000,000 shares par value $.10 a share - issued and outstanding 800,000 shares	80,000	80,000
Capital paid in excess of par value	560,000	560,000
Retained earnings	4,828,861	4,460,384
Total liabilities and stockholders equity	$11,681,738	$11,221,463

EXHIBIT 4 (Continued)

San Pablo Bottling Company

Income Statements

	1975	1974
Sales (net)	$22,703,229	$21,418,202
Cost of sales	15,208,914	14,234,814
Gross profit	7,494,315	7,183,388
Operating expenses		
Selling	4,140,600	3,983,762
Delivery	1,135,159	920,916
Administration (including depreciation expense)	1,211,736	1,212,645
Total operating expenses	6,487,495	6,117,323
Operating income	1,006,820	1,066,065
Interest expense	310,711	296,600
Income before taxes	696,109	769,465
Income taxes	327,632	362,843
NET Income	$ 368,477	$ 406,622

Case 3

ROLLINS MANUFACTURING CO., INC.

(Convertible Securities)

The Rollins Manufacturing Co., Inc., a producer of consumer hardware and industrial cleansing solvents and applicators, was founded in 1953 by Jonathan Rollins. For several years, the business was only marginally profitable. Finally, in 1958, profits improved significantly as the result of a long-term government contract to supply the military with specially formulated cleansing solvents to be used with electronic gear systems. However, despite the profitable six years, in 1964 Rollins decided to retire from business. Thus, when James Reed and Robert Hall approached Rollins regarding the possible sale of his firm, he was quite interested. By the end of the year the terms were finalized, and the operation changed leadership on January 1, 1965. In financing the enterprise, Reed and Hall provided approximately 69 percent of the equity with an additional 25,000 shares being purchased by other investors. (The total equity capital at that time was 80,500 shares of $1 par common stock.) However, in 1967, to acquire long-term financing for the purpose of financing growth, an additional 19,500 shares were placed with interested parties. Throughout the financial decision-making process, both Reed and Hall agree that maintaining in excess of 50 percent control is of key import to them.

In the year subsequent to the acquisition, Reed, as president of the firm, and Hall, as executive vice-president, undertook a study to determine the direction the firm should take in the future. The result was a 10-year plan for further expansion into recently developed cleansing solvents and accessories. In this light, the requisite for additional plant facilities became a pressing issue. The company purchased a building adaptable to its needs from John Bradshaw, the sole owner of a wholesale operation, who had recently become ill. After his illness, he began to liquidate the assets of the business and agreed to accept 5,000 shares of 4 percent preferred stock from the Rollins organization in payment for the building.

By 1966 the firm, under its new management, was experiencing excellent growth, and in five years had outgrown the facilities acquired from Bradshaw. Hence, in 1973, as the second phase in the 10-year expansion plan, the management issued $1,750,000 in 6 percent senior debt, having a maturity of 20 years. These funds were invested in additional plant and equipment for the expressed purpose of increasing production capacity in the following year.

Growth has continued to be excellent, and the need for additional capital equipment is again becoming a reality. The management of Rollins indicates that $750,000 is needed to meet the corporate financial requirements for the immediate future. These funds will be applied to the construction of facilities essential in meeting the obligations of a new government contract. To meet the terms of the contract, the plant must be started within three months. With this new addition, plant and equipment should be adequate for operations until 1980.

Sales in 1977 are expected to be 105 percent of 1976 sales, excluding revenues contributed by the new government contract. Cost of goods sold and operating expenses are expected to maintain the same percentages as experienced in 1976.

Reed contacted an investment banking firm for advice regarding the raising of the needed funds. After a study of the company, the banker recommended one of three alternatives to Reed:

1. Sell stock at $60 per share (current market value) less an approximate 10 percent for flotation costs. The current price/earnings ratio is considered by both management and the investment banker to be somewhat low in view of historical figures for both Rollins and the industry. Both groups feel that a return to a more normal price/earnings relative of 14.75 (based upon "fully diluted" earnings per share) will occur within the next six months. The 14.75 ratio is independent of future financing. Furthermore, the stock price should then continue to grow for several years at a 10 percent rate, after which a 6 percent rate could be expected.

2. Sell subordinated convertible debentures at a $1,000 market price with an 8 percent coupon rate and a 20-year life. Costs of underwriting and managing the issue would be 2.597 percent of the market price of the

security. The conversion ratio would "step down" as time elapses with the ratios being as follows:

Years	1- 3:	14.25
Years	4-10:	13.25
Years	11-20:	12.00

3. Sell subordinated convertible debentures at a $1,000 market price with a 7 percent coupon rate, maturing in 20 years and having a conversion price of $65. Flotation costs would be the same as the 8 percent debentures.

The call price for the convertibles in either alternative 2 or 3 will be as follows:

Years	Call Price
1-5	105
6-12	104
13-16	102
17-20	100

Rollins' outstanding senior debt is currently selling to yield 8 percent, while subordinated debentures having a risk class similar to the debentures under consideration, but without the conversion privilege, are selling at 10 percent. Also, the financial consultant recommends not executing the call feature until the conversion value exceeds the call price by 20 percent. Both Reed and Hall concur with such a policy.

QUESTIONS

1. From the perspective of Reed and Hall, which financing alternative should be undertaken?

2. What is the impact of each of the convertible issues upon the firm's earnings per share (both with and without the potential dilution effect being recognized)? In making your calculations, assume that the same percentage return on investment (before interest and taxes) can be achieved with the new funds as occurred in 1976 with existing assets. Also, assume the interest in 1977 will be equivalent to interest charges in 1976 if no financing occurs.

3. For alternative 2 (8 percent convertibles), determine as of the time of issue:

    a. the conversion value.

    b. "the bond-value floor," that is, the market price of the convertible issue when the conversion privilege is of no value due to a depressed common stock price.

    c. the premium-over-conversion value and the premium-over-bond value.

4. a. Why is a "step-down" conversion ratio employed?

   b. In view of the firm's call policy and the expected price movement, when would the issue be called? Answer in terms of both market price of the issue and approximate time.

   c. What would you expect the premium-over-conversion value and bond value to be at the time the issue is called?

   d. Experience shows that as the conversion value falls to approximately 50 percent of the "bond-value floor," the market value of a convertible debenture essentially becomes equivalent to the floor. In this context, compute both premiums if the anticipated increase in the stock price did not materialize but rather decreased to a low of $24.

5. With the results from the previous questions, develop a graph at the expected time of the call that reflects the *approximate* relationships between (1) the bond-value floor, the conversion value, and the market value of the 8 percent convertible debentures, and (2) the price of the common stock. (Let the vertical axis comprise the market, bond, and conversion value of the convertible security, while the horizontal axis depicts the price of the common stock.)

6. Based upon the prior computations, explain the reasons for the premium-over-conversion value and the premium-over-bond value. Also, explain the relationship of the two premiums.

EXHIBIT 1

Rollins Manufacturing Co., Inc.

Income Statements
1972-1976

	1976	1975	1974	1973	1972
Sales	$9,000,000	$8,460,000	$8,100,000	$4,057,500	$3,367,000
Costs of goods sold	4,050,000	3,785,850	3,240,000	1,704,150	1,438,800
Gross profit	4,950,000	4,674,150	4,860,000	2,353,350	1,928,200
Operating expenses[1]	3,939,620	3,715,690	3,962,422	1,804,963	1,604,200
Earnings before interest and taxes	1,010,380	958,460	897,578	548,387	324,000
Interest	129,220	129,290	138,530	150,710	35,000
Taxable income	881,160	829,170	759,048	397,677	289,000
Taxes[2]	416,457	391,502	357,843	184,385	180,220
Income after taxes	464,703	437,668	401,205	213,292	108,780
Preferred dividends	20,000	20,000	20,000	20,000	20,000
Earnings available to common	444,703	417,668	381,205	193,292	88,780
Earnings per share	$4.45	$4.18	$3.81	$1.93	$ .89

[1] Include $225,000 in depreciation charges for 1976.

[2] Tax rate: 22 percent for 0 - $25,000; 48 percent for over $25,000.

EXHIBIT 2

Rollins Manufacturing Co., Inc.

Balance Sheets ($000)
1972-1976

	1976	1975	1974	1973	1972
Cash	$ 550	$ 500	$ 450	$ 400	$ 300
Accounts receivable	850	700	600	450	500
Marketable securities	200	150	150	150	50
Inventories	1,000	800	700	650	500
Net plant and equipment	2,400	2,550	2,600	2,700	1,250
Total assets	5,000	4,700	4,500	4,350	2,600
Trade payables	$ 250	$ 250	$ 200	$ 200	$ 400
Short-term notes (7%)	96	97	229	403	500
Long-term bonds (7%)	1,750	1,750	1,750	1,750	0
Preferred stock (4%)	500	500	500	500	500
Common stock par					
($1 par)	100	100	100	100	100
Capital surplus	900	900	900	900	900
Retained earnings	1,404	1,103	821	497	200
Total liabilities					
and equity	$5,000	$4,700	$4,500	$4,350	$2,600

Selected 1976 Industry Norms:
Current ratio:	4.00X
Return on assets	
(before interest and taxes):	17.5%
Total debt/total assets:	35%
Preferred/total assets:	5%
Return on common:	15%

Case 4

BARRINGER FABRICATORS, INC.

(Refunding a Bond Issue)

Seven years ago, Barringer Fabricators, Inc. entered the tire recapping business by acquiring an old line recapping firm. Since that time, Barringer has expanded its recapping operations with major inroads being made into the "off-the-road" vehicle field. In March, Barringer reported $1.15 per share for the fiscal year just ended, with over 85 percent of its sales attributable to the firm's recapping operations.

Prospects for future growth look particularly good for Barringer in light of the fact that the firm holds exclusive rights to a newly patented "hot capping" process (Bondtread), which, according to informed industry sources, will revolutionize the off-the-road tire recapping business. Bondtread boasts lower cost and roughly the same performance characteristics as the conventional "cold process." The new process achieves its cost savings through the use of a less expensive rubber compound and through reduced handling. The tire is coated, bonded, and patterned in a single revolution through the machine.

Barringer's recapping business has led to a marked improvement in the financial posture of the firm over the past five years. In conjunction with the company's improved financial stature, the general easing of credit conditions has resulted in a drastic lowering in the cost of borrowed funds to the firm. In May 1970, for example, Barringer issued $10 million in first mortgage bonds. These bonds carried a 9¼ percent rate of interest and were not callable for a period of five years after issuance.[1] In the five years since the bond issue, Barringer's bond rating has improved from Baa to A (Moody's Investor Service). Combined, these factors have resulted in a lowering of the cost of new debt to an estimated 8 percent.

EXHIBIT 1

The outstanding issue had the following characteristics:

Coupon rate	9¼ percent
Par value	$1,000.00
Issue size	$10 million
Due date	May 15, 2000
Call premium	One year's interest in the first year in which the bonds are callable and declining by ½ percent per year until the 18th year, and zero thereafter.
Unamortized discount	$500,000.00
Unamortized issue expense	$100,000.00

The corresponding characterisitcs of the refunding issue are as follows:

Coupon rate	8 percent
Par value (also the price at which the bonds are expected to be sold)	$1,000.00
Due date	May 15, 2000
Underwriters spread	1½ percent of the face value of the issue plus a $400,000 fee
Overlap period (during which time both the old and new issues will be outstanding)	2 months
Return on treasury bill investment during the overlap period	6 percent

The lower cost of new debt funds was brought to the attention of Barringer's management by the investment banking house that handled the 1970 bond issue. The rather substantial (125 basis point) reduction in borrowing cost along with the expiration of the five-year delayed call on the outstanding issue, according to the investment banker, make the refunding of the issue worth considering by Barringer. Since Barringer has never refunded a public offering,

[1]Pertinent information regarding the outstanding issue and the refunding issue is found in Exhibit 1.

the firm's management has a number of serious questions and misgivings concerning both how the refunding should be analyzed and whether it should be undertaken even if it is found to be profitable.

J. J. Bows, Barringer's financial vice-president, felt that the refunding probably would be profitable, but was concerned over the path of interest rates in the months to come. His chief concern was that the firm would give up the opportunity to refund at a more desirable time in the future if delayed-call bonds were sold at the present time. The firm had had to live for five years with the 9¼ percent bonds due to the delayed call provision, and Bows wanted to be very sure that the firm was making the right move before any action was taken.

Bows' assistant, Jerry Wilson, was not convinced that the current refunding was in the best interests of the firm. This belief was founded on the fact that Barringer had just approved a record $20 million capital budget for fiscal year 1975. Wilson felt that the proposed refunding of a $10 million bond issue, along with the need to enter the capital market for an added $15 million to help finance the planned capital expenditures, would be viewed as excessive by the market and could result in a higher cost of funds to the firm. A second assistant to the financial vice-president, Jim Koss, indicated that the refunding should not affect the other capital raising plans of the firm since the total financing of the company would not be altered. In fact, if anything, the refunding should improve the ability of the firm to raise the needed funds since the new issue would be less expensive.

Bows suggested that the profitability of refunding be analyzed using the net present value technique used by the firm in making capital investment decisions. However, he was not sure whether Barringer's after-tax cost of capital (approximately 10 percent) or some other rate, such as the after-tax, risk-free rate (the current before-tax yield on 90-day U.S. treasury bills is 6 percent) should be used in discounting the cash flows. Even if refunding now were found to be profitable, Bows questioned whether the refunding should be delayed until the path of future interest rates could be determined.

Based on their discussion of the proposed refunding, the two assistants to the financial vice-president were asked to prepare a recommendation as to whether the refunding should be undertaken. The analysts specifically were asked to address their report to the appropriate rate of discount for the refunding cash flows and the timing problem.

QUESTIONS

1. What rate of discount is appropriate to refunding cash flows? Explain.
2. Compute the net present value of refunding at the present time. You may assume a 50 percent marginal income tax rate.
3. How can the problem of selecting the optimal time for the refunding be solved? Discuss the feasibility of successfully timing the issuance of new bonds to obtain the maximum interest savings from the refunding.

Case 5

A. G. CRAFFORD INDUSTRIES

(Lease versus Borrow Decision)

Founded in 1957 and headquartered in Birmingham, Alabama, A.G. Crafford Industries operates six metal service centers located throughout the southeastern United States. Last year, based on annual sales of $29.4 million, the company realized earnings per share of $1, which represents an increase of more than 14 percent from one year earlier (see Exhibit 1). This increase in earnings represents a continuation in the growth that AGCI has experienced for the past five years.

AGCI acts essentially as a middleman between mill and manufacturer. Each of its service centers maintains a diverse inventory of galvanized and stainless steel pipe and sheet metal, as well as a variety of aluminum and nickel alloys. Recent growth in the industry largely can be attributed to the increasing demand for small custom orders, which the mills have chosen not to satisfy in lieu of larger and more profitable orders.

AGCI has recently made the decision to acquire a new computer system to be used in inventory control for its six plant locations, as well as performing the firm's general accounting functions. In the past, inventory control has been largely handled by each service center; however, with the increase in interest rates AGCI's management feels that a centralized inventory control system can provide substantial cost savings through reduced duplication and increased control. The decision to acquire the system has been finalized, including the specific hardware and software configuration needed; however, the firm has not determined the best method for financing the acquisition.

EXHIBIT 1

A. G. Crafford Industries

Balance Sheet
12/31/77

Assets

Cash	$ 1,244,000
Accounts Receivable	6,387,000
Inventories	16,131,000
Total Current Assets	23,762,000
Plant and Equipment	21,046,000
less: Accumulated Depreciation	9,641,000
Net Plant and Equipment	11,405,000
Total Assets	$35,167,000

Liabilities and Stockholders Equity

Acccounts Payable	$ 680,000
Notes Payable	1,500,000
Taxes Payable	312,000
Other payables	2,416,000
Total Current Liabilities	4,908,000
First Mortgage bonds (6's 1986)	7,500,000
Subordinated debentures (8's 1990)	5,000,000
Total Long-term Debt	12,500,000
Common stock ($1 par)	1,200,000
Paid-in-Capital	3,400,000
Retained Earnings	13,159,000
Total Common Equity	17,759,000
Total Liabilities and Stockholders Equity	$35,167,000

Income Statement
For the Year Ended
12/31/75

Net Sales	$29,412,000
Cost of Sales	23,046,000
Gross Profit	6,366,000
Operating Expenses:	
Wages and Salaries	1,401,000
Administrative Expense	748,000
Depreciation	942,000
Total Operating Expenses	3,091,000
Net Operating Income	3,275,000
Interest Expense	975,000
Net Income Before Taxes	2,300,000
Taxes Payable	1,097,000
Net Income	1,203,000

The manufacturer of the computer system will either sell the system or lease it under a long-term agreement. The lease alternative looks particularly attractive to AGCI's management in light of the firm's heavy use of financial leverage in the past. In fact, AGCI's management feels that a long-term debt to total capitalization ratio of 40 to 45 percent is deemed acceptable within the industry.

Upon receiving the buyer's request for the acquisition of the system, the firm's chief financial officer, James M. Tarver, called in his chief assistant to discuss the leasing-borrowing alternative. Tarver asked that his assistant provide a complete report as to the relative merits of the two proposals by the end of the week. The assistant to the treasurer, William L. Simpson, immediately called in two of his financial analysts to discuss the problem. He instructed the analysts to work up independent reports on the costs of the alternative financing methods and to have them on his desk by Wednesday so that he could make his final recommendation to Tarver by Thursday afternoon.

Before the meeting was adjourned, a number of issues were raised concerning the proper means for addressing the problem. Among the items mentioned was the problem associated with adjusting the annual costs of the alternatives to their present value. The rate used in analyzing asset acquisitions was the firm's cost of capital, which was estimated to be approximately 12 percent. One of the analysts expressed the opinion that this rate was too high since it reflected a risk premium associated with the types of asset acquisitions normally made by the firm, and the present problem was a financing decision, not an acquisition problem. Alternative discount rates obviously included the risk-free rate, which was currently 6 percent before taxes (rate on short-term U.S. treasury obligations), the cost of borrowed funds (the firm had a commitment for the necessary funds from its bank at 8 percent), or perhaps some other rate falling between the risk-free rate and the cost of capital.

Simpson gave each of the analysts the following cost information for the two financing choices:

Purchase price of the computer system	$100,000
Estimated useful life	5 years
Estimated salvage value	20,000
Annual lease expense (including the maintenance contract)[1]	22,000

Also, for purposes of analysis, the members were told to use straight line depreciation.

---

[1]The lease agreement includes a maintenance contract valued by AGCI at $6,000 per annum. Also, the lease and maintenance payments are made at the beginning of each year, whereas loan payments are to be made at the end of the year.

QUESTIONS

1. As an analyst faced with preparing a report on the costs of the two financing arrangements, what rate or rates of discount do you feel are appropriate to the lease-borrow problem? Support your answer with appropriate reasons.

2. Should the leasing arrangement be accepted? Explain.

3. How will the firm's final decision affect its financial risk and consequently its cost of capital? Explain.

Case 6

COMMONWEALTH BUSINESS INSTRUMENTS

(Long-Term Financing Choices)

Rick Leach was hired by Commonwealth Business Instruments (CBI) 10 months ago as an assistant to comptroller Doug Fisher. Since that time his main task has been an analysis of the profitability of CBI's various products. At the completion of this project, Leach asked to be given a more challenging assignment, and as a result, on December 1, 1975, he was given the task of analyzing the various proposals that have been suggested for raising $28 million in additional funds in the capital market needed for the production and promotion of some new products.

CBI was founded in Ann Arbor, Michigan, in 1894 by Rhodes Baker to produce manual typewriters. Through the 1920s CBI grew at a rapid pace, expanding its product line to include manual calculators and improving and expanding its typewriter line. With the business slowdown of the 1930s, CBI's growth stopped and did not begin moving again until the early 1950s. At that time CBI went through a major change in both its management personnel and its product line, resulting in five years of strong company growth. Electric typewriters and calculators replaced the manual counterparts as CBI's major products, and extensive research was made into computer applications in these fields. After 10 years of moderate stagnation in sales, this research paid off in the late 1960s resulting in a strong growth pattern once again. This growth pattern was largely a result of CBI's increased emphasis in the calculator market.

Although the new growth was encouraging, it has not been overly stable, especially during the 1974 recession when CBI's earnings dropped sharply. As a result of this profit instability, CBI had in recent years a low price-earnings ratio relative to other growth stocks in the market, in spite of the fact that CBI had shown above average growth during the past seven years (see Exhibits 1 and 2). However, from discussions with several Wall Street analysts, Fisher has come to believe that if CBI can show a strong comeback from the 1974 slowdown, indicating that it has returned to its earning ways of the past several years, the stock will be looked upon favorably by investors. This could perhaps result in a doubling of the firm's price-earnings ratio. As the current need for funds is directly related to CBI's movement into the mini and desk computer field, it is felt that these products will generate the strong earnings necessary to boost CBI's share price substantially. For this reason, Fisher is somewhat hesitant about issuing additional common stock at a price that is, in his opinion, temporarily depressed. He feels that if the issuance of common stock can be postponed for two years, the stock price may well be doubled, allowing CBI to raise the required capital by issuing only half the number of shares currently required to raise the necessary capital. Fisher felt quite confident that this, in fact, would be the case, as the 1976 expected level of EBIT was $16 million, while the 1978 expected level of EBIT was $22 million and there was only a minor chance (10 percent) of nonacceptance of the new mini and desk calculator. If the mini and desk calculator meet this resistance, it is estimated that the 1978 EBIT could not fall below $14 million. Moreover, Fisher has stated that to reach an acceptable price earnings level, the company has adopted a firm policy of not lowering dividends per share regardless of the profit level in that year, in an attempt to make the stock more appealing to institutional investors.

EXHIBIT 1

Comparative NYSE-ASE Price-Earning Ratios

Year	CBI's Average P-E Ratio	NYSE-ASE Average P-E Ratio	NYSE-ASE Average P-E Ratio for Companies Exhibiting a 20% Compound Growth Rate in EPS over the Past Seven Years.
1975	16.76	9.53	31.46
1974	11.64	6.91	25.24
1973	19.81	17.46	37.42
1972	20.16	19.22	39.25
1971	19.74	18.72	38.91
1970	17.60	17.64	38.71
1969	15.63	17.26	36.12
1968	14.91	17.80	35.56

EXHIBIT 2

CBI's Stock Performance

Year	Average Common Stock Price	Earning/Share	Dividend/Share
1975	$60.00	3.58	1.00
1974	30.61	2.63	.90
1973	64.97	3.28	.88
1972	53.42	2.65	.74
1971	41.85	2.12	.60
1970	29.39	1.67	.47
1969	20.32	1.30	.37
1968	15.21	1.02	.29

Complicating the financing question is the fact that CBI currently has proportionally more debt in its capital structure than do other companies in the same industry (see Exhibit 3). Through conversation with Fisher, Rick Leach learned that even though interest rates appeared to be at an attractive level, falling substantially from their 1974 peaks, and while it would be possible to raise current funds through the issuance of long-term debt, Fisher feels that this would prohibit the issuance of any additional debt prior to a substantial increase in equity capital and would thereby reduce CBI's future financing flexibility. This is due to the potentially unfavorable effect of excess long-term debt on CBI's bond rating and its common stock price. CBI's long-term debt problem is magnified by the fact that the company in effect considers preferred stock as a form of subordinated debt, refusing ever to pass a preferred stock dividend.

The decision as to how to finance the $28 million in new funds is further complicated because in three years it will be necessary for CBI again to tap the financial markets for an additional $28 million. Although the need for current funds is related to CBI's movement into the mini and desk computer market, the additional funds needed in three years will be primarily related to the company's introduction and promotion of product line improvements.

EXHIBIT 3

Comparative Capital Structures

Capital Structure	Dec. 1, 1975	Industry Average, Business Instruments Companies Dec. 1, 1975
Debt	52%	45%
Preferred Stock	14%	15%
Common Stock and Earned Surplus	34%	40%

Currently, CBI has several improved automatic copy-typewriters nearing the final development stage. Production for these products is not scheduled to begin until early 1979, but $28 million in outside funding will be needed in three years to purchase the specialized production equipment. This possibly could be postponed somewhat and introduced at a slower speed, which would quite possibly allow competition to develop substitutes, thus drastically reducing the potential profitability of the product.

While CBI was planning on engaging the services of an investment banker in offering their proposed issue to the public, they have decided to solicit the services of an investment banker on a competitive bid basis rather than a negotiated bid basis. Thus, it will be necessary for CBI to assemble the new offering prior to inviting bids from investment bankers. After CBI has assembled the security package, they will sell it to an investment banker, who will in turn sell the securities to the public. With this in mind, Fisher has already solicited the

EXHIBIT 4

Balance Sheet
As of Dec. 1, 1975
(Dollars Figures in Thousands)

Assets

Cash	$ 10,000
Accounts Receivable	14,000
Inventory	29,000
Total Current Assets	53,000
Fixed Assets, net	56,000
Deferred Charges	1,000
Total Assets	110,000

Liabilities

Accounts Payable	1,300
Accruals	1,200
Taxes Payable	1,500
Total Current Liabilities	4,000
Long term debt outstanding	55,000
(Sold at par due 1999, 6.0%, no sinking fund requirements)	
Preferred Stock	15,000
($6.00 cumulative, $100 par)	
Common Stock (985,000 shares outstanding)	985
Paid-In-Capital	15,015
Retained Earnings	20,000
Total Liabilities and Net Worth	110,000

opinion of several of his staff members as to the appropriate design of the new issue and has compiled a list of four possible alternatives. It is Leach's job to review and evaluate these alternatives critically and provide Fisher with a recommended strategy for raising the necessary funds in the capital market.

The four alternatives to be evaluated by Rick Leach are as follows:

1. Rather than offer common stock directly to the public, CBI could offer the new common stock to the current shareholders on a privileged subscription basis. This action is not required by CBI's corporate charter, but it has been argued by several of Fisher's assistants that as the common stock is currently selling for what is considered a depressed price, this would allow existing shareholders to maintain their proportionate ownership or benefit from the sale of the rights, thus keeping the shareholders happy. Under this proposal CBI would issue additional stock through a rights offering with a price of $48 per share. The expected flotation costs would amount to approximately $1 per share for each share successfully subscribed to.

2. Alternatively, CBI could offer common stock directly to the public. Under this plan, new shares would be sold to the public at a price of $57 per share with underwriting costs amounting to $2 per share.

3. A third possibility for raising new funds is through the issue of 10-year 5½ percent nonconvertible debentures. These could be issued at par with 2 percent of the par value going to the investment banker in return for performing the tasks of distribution and underwriting the issue. This issue would include a sinking fund requirement of $4,000,000 per year

EXHIBIT 5

C.B.I Corporation

Statement of Income
Fiscal Year Ended Dec. 1, 1975
(In Thousands)

Net Sales	$ 77,462
Cost of Goods Sold	53,524
Selling, General Administrative	11,782
EBIT	12,156
Interest	3,300
Income before Taxes	8,856
Taxes	4,428
Earnings after Taxes	4,428
Preferred Stock Dividends	900
Earnings available to Common Stockholders	3,528
Shares Outstanding (985,000)	985
Earnings per Common Share (in dollars)	$3.58

due every year, with the first payment due three years after the issue was floated.

4. Finally, CBI could raise their needed funds through the issuance of 10-year 5 percent convertible subordinated debentures callable at 107, which could be sold at par with 2 percent of the par value going to the investment banker in return for services. These bonds would be convertible at $75 a share after one year. This conversion price would hold for two years and then rise to $90 per share, and subsequently increase $10 per share every three years until maturity. If the bonds were not converted after three years, a sinking fund requirement of $4,000,000 per year would become effective.

Leach was given two days to prepare his recommended strategy as to the proper method CBI should undertake to raise the necessary funds in the capital market. He was instructed by Fisher to consider the obvious risk-return tradeoffs in addition to the effect of the current decision on future financing.

QUESTIONS

1. What factors should be considered in making the financing decision faced by CBI? Discuss each briefly.

2. To raise the needed $28 million, how many shares of stock must be sold under the rights offering proposal, assuming all shares are subscribed?

3. Compute the number of rights required to buy a share of stock.

4. Compute the value of a right when the stock is selling at $60 per share rights on.

5. Compute the value of the stock when it goes exrights.

6. Is it likely they will all be exercised?

7. Under alternative 2, how many new shares of common stock must be issued to raise the needed $28 million?

8. What is the initial conversion ratio of the convertibles proposed in alternative 4?

9. What is the initial conversion value of each debenture? What is the meaning of this value?

10. How many shares must be issued if all debentures are converted at the initial conversion price?

11. What is the purpose of the stepped-up conversion prices?

12. For the EBIT level of $16 million, calculate the EPS for each of the alternative methods of financing: Assume a 50% tax rate and that conversion of the convertibles (a) has not taken place, and (b) has taken place at the $75 conversion price.

13. Examine the interest coverage ratio for 1976 and 1978 assuming the expected EBIT level in 1976 of $16,000,000 and for 1978 the expected

EBIT level of $22,000,000 and the minimum possible level of $14,000,000. Are there any modifications in this ratio that might be interesting? If additional information were available, what other ratios might be interesting?

14. Which financing alternative identified in the case would serve the best interests of CBI? Might any other methods be considered?

Section 6

Noteworthy
Financial
Management
Problems

Case 1

TRANER FURNITURE COMPANY

(Dividend Policy)

The Traner Furniture Company (TFC) is a diversified manufacturer of household furnishings located in Rocky Mount, North Carolina. The firm's expansion program, begun in the early 1960s, has been continued to the point where the company is now represented in most major furniture lines that have national appeal. About 55 percent of sales for the company are generated by its lines of wooden furniture; the other 45 percent are attributed to its upholstered products. Throughout all of its product lines, TFC has been able to offer very high quality for every dollar spent by consumers. TFC's many competitors praise its quality control and point to it as a major reason for the organization's solid reputation in the industry.

That reputation is buttressed by a pervasive respect among both competing manufacturers and security analysts for the leadership and overall managerial abilities of John Collberg, president of TFC. Collberg has unique sales and styling talents that almost provide him with a mystique in the furniture profession. These attributes allow him to run the affairs of this publicly held corporation quite sternly.

It is Monday, and Collberg has his executive staff preparing for the quarterly meeting of the board of directors, which will take place on Friday. Several economic developments directly affecting the financial picture for TFC are disturbing its chief executive officer. Alan Boyer, the head purchasing agent for the company, today presented Collberg with the information shown in Exhibit 1. Boyer felt certain that, on the average, a 10 percent price rise in the various woods used in quantity by TFC would be experienced during the next fiscal year.

EXHIBIT 1

Traner Furniture Company

Wood Price Increases

Division	Location	Key Products	Wood Inputs	Projected Price Rise
Maplemount	Greenwood, N.C.	Quality re-cliners	Hackberry, plywood, oak	15%
Hazeldown	Dublin, Ga.	Juvenile furniture	Oak, pine	8%
Ballett	Ballett, Va.	Bedroom, dining room	Poplar, oak, tupelo, hack-berry	8%
Hickory Style	Hickory, N.C.	Upholstered furniture	Mixed hardwoods	9%
Victoria	Wellsville, Pa.	Correlated tables	Mahogany, pecan	12%

Because of the firm's total commitment to quality merchandise, Collberg would not hear of using some cheaper grades of lumber to dampen the effect of the price increases expected by the purchasing department. "A few cracked frames, and there goes 70 years worth of reputation," he argued.

After Boyer's information reached Collberg, J. R. Wilson discussed with the company president the prospects for interest rate levels over the coming year. Wilson is the vice-president of finance for TFC. During the past month of October, Wilson had digested numerous governmental reports, commercial and Federal Reserve bank letters, and brokerage house publications that touched upon interest rate projections for next year. The composite tone of these forecasts was not at all good for the furniture industry. Wilson put together his own projections, influenced by the materials that he had been examining, and offered them to Collberg in the form of Exhibit 2.

EXHIBIT 2

Traner Furniture Company

Recent Interest Rate Levels and Forecasts

Time	3-Month Treasury Bills	Prime Bankers' Acceptances	4-6 Month Commercial Paper
Current year[1]	7.04%	8.08%	8.15%
One year ago	4.07	4.47	4.69
Two years ago	4.35	4.85	5.11
Three years ago	6.46	7.31	7.72
Next July	7.53%	11.77%	11.80%
Next August	8.80	12.07	11.60
Next September	8.82	11.47	11.58

[1]Includes 11 months of actual data and a forecast for December.

Wilson's prognostication did not please Collberg. Interest rate levels are extraordinarily critical to the furniture manufacturing industry.

"Look at this!" Collberg yelled as he pushed a table (Exhibit 3) of figures in front of the vice-president. "I just received this from the Regional Furniture Manufacturers' Association."

EXHIBIT 3

Traner Furniture Company

Housing Starts
New Private Housing Units Authorized[1]
(Seasonally Adjusted Annual Rates in Thousands)

January -	2,233	May -	1,838	September -	1,596
February -	2,209	June -	2,030	October -	1,316
March -	2,129	July -	1,780	November -	1,314
April -	1,939	August -	1,750	December -	1,231

[1]Authorized by issuance of local building permits for the current year; the December figure is preliminary.

Collberg's usually calm and totally composed manner disintegrated as he informed Wilson that the Manufacturers' Association was projecting annual new housing starts at a rate below 1 million units for the first quarter of next year.

This would be the lowest rate since late 1966, if the forecast proved true, and a startling 60 percent below the rate that culminated the 1970-1973 housing boom.

"I'll need the fiscal year financial statements by tomorrow along with your projection of sales, net income, and earnings per share for each of the four quarters of next year," Collberg told Wilson. "We need to make a firm recommendation to the board of directors as to our most prudent dividend policy in the light of these developments."

Collberg reminded Wilson of the executive staff's decision to increase its hourly wage schedule at the Virginia and North Carolina production facilities. As labor is somewhat tight in both of these states, the top management of TFC decided to offer higher wages than some of the competition to attract a steady supply of help.

Wilson left the president's office and signaled for Barney Abbott to enter. As he did so, he quickly moved his right index finger in a semicircular motion across his throat, giving Abbott advance warning of Collberg's general mood. Abbott is now in his 10th year of service to TFC as its corporate attorney. Collberg gave Abbott a copy of a letter that he had received from a shareholder who was expressing displeasure with TFC's dividend policy (Exhibit 4). Collberg said he was unaware that the retention of earnings could be deemed "improper" by the courts. He instructed Abbott to determine whether TFC should be concerned with the implications of the letter received from Adam Randolph.

By Tuesday noon Collberg's staff had on his desk considerable information pointed toward the question of the firm's dividend policy. As he poured over this data (Exhibits 5-10), Collberg became certain that several problems related to the formulation of next year's dividend policy would be touched upon at the director's meeting. Some members of the board would seize upon the letter from Adam Randolph to further their cause for an increase in the annual cash dividend. Others would argue strongly for a cut in the cash dividend payout. Another group could be counted on to favor keeping the current 69 cent dividend intact. Finally, some board members from all of these camps would argue strongly against the company's policy of paying a regular quarterly dividend of 14 cents; the remainder has been the declaration of an extra dividend at year end. TFC has followed this procedure the past five years. Those against it feel that the "extra" portion of the dividend should be built into the regular quarterly payment.

PROBLEMS

1. Prepare a table that contains yearly price/earnings ratios, dividend payout ratios, and market value to book value ratios for TFC and its three main competitors.

EXHIBIT 4

Mr. John Collberg, President
Traner Furniture Company
Rocky Mount, North Carolina

Dear Mr. Collberg:

I have been a small investor in TFC common shares for approximately three years. It disturbs me that you and your board of directors continue to follow such a highly conservative dividend payout policy as has been evidenced by the recent past.

In light of (1) your firm's extreme liquidity, (2) low level of long-term debt, and (3) high executive compensation level, I believe that TFC is a prime candidate for the accumulated earnings tax. It seems to me that an increase in the cash dividend would be more beneficial to the firm's owners than having to prove in tax court that TFC has not been improperly accumulating surplus.

Sometimes I think the management of TFC continues to act like it is a family held enterprise rather than a public company whose shares are actively traded over-the-counter.

Sincerely,

Adam Randolph
Upper Vista, Virginia

CC: Internal Revenue Service
      Southeast Region
      Memphis, Tennessee

2.   Compute compound annual growth rates in earnings per share for TFC and competitors. Use

$$\frac{\text{EPS current year}}{\text{EPS 4 years ago}}$$

to develop appropriate interest factors; then convert these interest factors to approximate (and appropriate) growth rates in earnings per share.

3.   Compute a five-year composite dividend payout ratio for TFC and competitors by evaluating

$$\sum_{T=1}^{5} D_t/E_t$$

where D_t is cash dividend paid during time period t, and E_t is earnings per share during time period t.

EXHIBIT 5

Traner Furniture Company

Selected Financial Statistics (Traner and Competitors)
(Per Share Basis)

Item	4 Years Ago	3 Years Ago	2 Years Ago	1 Year Ago	Current Year
Traner					
Cash dividends	$ .59	$ .61	$ .61	$ .65	$ .69
Earnings	1.58	2.03	2.12	2.79	2.71
Book value	15.69	17.14	18.62	20.77	22.67
Share price (mid-point of yearly high-low range)	26.46	40.18	43.60	25.48	16.17
Barttonn South					
Cash dividends	$ .63	$ .86	$ 1.01	$ .98	$ .98
Earnings	1.36	1.90	1.99	1.93	1.48
Book value	10.18	11.23	12.23	13.17	13.95
Share price	23.03	43.61	47.53	29.89	16.66
Harbor Groupings					
Cash dividends	$ .29	$ .32	$ .33	$ .34	$ .35
Earnings	.90	.72	.99	1.21	1.64
Book value	5.89	6.29	6.94	7.80	9.08
Share price	14.70	20.09	20.09	12.25	9.80
Sleepy-Boy					
Cash dividends	$ .23	$ .29	$ .29	$ .34	$ .39
Earnings	.76	1.14	1.30	1.68	1.54
Book value	4.16	5.02	6.93	8.30	9.47
Share price	43.12	22.05	37.73	26.95	9.31

4. Recall that the growth rate in the Gordon valuation and cost of capital model can be represented by G = b r, where b is the fraction of current earnings retained and r is the productivity of those retentions. Using information derived from the previous two questions, calculate the implied productivity of retentions for the subject firms.

5. Considering all data, make a recommendation as to the proper *payout ratio* for TFC to strive to maintain over longer periods, and as to the *size* of the dividend for each of the four quarters of next year.

EXHIBIT 6

Traner Furniture Company

Selected Financial Ratios
(Traner and Competitors)
(Latest 12 Months)

Item	Traner	Barttonn South	Harbor Groupings	Sleepy-Boy
Net working capital per share	$14.21	$ 8.24	$ 5.59	$ 6.31
Current ratio	8.60 X	7.75 X	4.01 X	3.98 X
Long-term debt to total equity	1.4%	3.3%	20.7%	11.6%
Inventory turnover (COS/ EI)	4.56 X	4.61 X	4.23 X	3.75 X
Return on equity (net income/ total equity)	11.8%	10.7%	17.7%	16.4%
Return on assets (net income/ total assets)	10.8%	9.6%	12.3%	12.2%

EXHIBIT 7

Traner Furniture Company

Income Statement
End of Current Fiscal Year

Net sales	$ 119,664,250
Cost of sales	- 84,701,301
Gross profit	$ 34,962,949
Selling and administrative expenses	- 21,539,806
Operating income	$ 13,423,143
Other income and expenses:	
Income from investments	555,450
Interest expense	- 59,436
Miscellaneous, net	234,472
Earnings before taxes	$ 14,153,629
Taxes (federal and state)	- 6,820,800
Net income	$ 7,332,829
Preferred dividends paid	- 51,195
Earnings available to common	$ 7,281,634

EXHIBIT 8

Traner Furniture Company

Balance Sheet
End of Current Fiscal Year

Assets

Cash	$ 846,312
Marketable securities	8,340,782
Accounts receivable	14,785,326
Inventories	18,572,714
Prepaid expenses	668,927
Total current assets	$ 43,214,061
Net property and equipment	21,693,493
Other assets	2,886,630
Total assets	$ 67,794,184

Liabilities and Stockholders' Equity

Total current liabilities	$ 5,027,185
Long-term debt	840,245
Stockholders' equity:	
Preferred stock	1,023,904
Common stock (2,686,950 shares)	13,193,250
Paid in surplus	3,736,582
Retained earnings	44,435,084
Treasury stock	- 462,066
Total stockholders' equity	$ 61,926,754
Total liabilities and equity	$ 67,794,184

EXHIBIT 9

Traner Furniture Company

Comparative Annual Remuneration for Top Officers

Position	Traner	Average of 3 Main Competitors
President	$133,468	$105,756
Financial vice-president	89,389	88,420
Marketing vice-president	88,404	64,555

EXHIBIT 10

Traner Furniture Company

Selected Financial Projections
Next Year

Item	First Quarter	Second Quarter
Sales	$22,965,000	$21,729,000
Net income	784,800	1,099,000
Earnings per share	$ 0.29	$ 0.41

Item	Third Quarter	Fourth Quarter
Sales	$28,741,000	$27,614,000
Net income	2,289,000	2,312,000
Earnings per share	$ 0.85	$ 0.86

Case 2

MARRIOTT PETROLEUM CORPORATION

(Mergers and Acquisitions)

The Marriott Petroleum Corporation is a partially integrated oil company that explores for, produces, refines, and markets petroleum and petroleum products. The corporation was organized in 1939, and is currently traded in the over-the-counter market.

The history of the company dates back to Thomas Marriott, a student from the University of Nebraska who arrived in Ponca City, Louisiana, in 1927. His professional goal at that time was to revolutionize the oil industry through the latest developments in petroleum geology. After conducting extensive technical research, he leased land that he considered to be the most promising in terms of oil reserves. Drawing upon his own limited financing, he immediately began a drilling program. At first, his efforts proved to be disappointing; however, as his funds were quickly approaching complete depletion, a large pay load was discovered, which proved to be the foundation of the firm's financial welfare. In 1939 the enterprise was incorporated under the name of Marriott Petroleum Corporation. It has grown successfully throughout the years, maturing into one of the more successful smaller petroleum companies.

Historically, the corporate efforts in oil and gas exploration have primarily been concentrated throughout the southwestern states of Texas, Oklahoma, Arkansas, and Louisiana. In exploring for such natural resources, Marriott has, on several occasions, been responsible for innovations in drilling. For instance, company researchers have experimented with lasers, electric sparks, and shaped charges. Additionally, exploration teams are implementing high presssure jets, which offer substantial improvement for injecting mud, an essential ingredient in the drilling process, through the drill bit nozzle. Moreover, Marriott has been engaged in the active search for new oil and gas reserves in the Gulf of Mexico, near Yucatan, Old Mexico. In these latter efforts in the Gulf, a significant portion of the research has been directed toward exploration of the ocean waters through the application of computer technology. Techniques have been developed for analyzing, modeling, and mapping geological and geophysical data and for solving complex seismic ray-path problems in three dimensions. Also, Marriott has made advances in offshore drilling methods centering around the fixation of a drill ship over a particular location in the water. The new approach combines (1) satellite navigation, thereby determining the vessel location; (2) an acoustic beacon to find the ship's position relative to the sea floor; and (3) a computer-controlled thruster propulsion system to control ship movement.

In addition to the petroleum field, Marriott is engaged in several other operations. These divisions, mostly originating within the past 10 years, include:

1. *The production of coal.* In recent years, the research department has made several breakthroughs in the area of coal production. Such innovations have included a new process for making substitute hydrocarbon fuels from coal; an improved method for producing pollution-free blast furnace coke from coal; and a revolutionary process for the production of clean, synthetic fuels derived from coal.

2. *Industrial chemicals.* Another area of Marriott's involvement is the supplying of industrial chemicals for use in biodegradable detergents and vinyl plastics. The company's major chemical complex, located in Ruskmore, Louisiana, derives hydrocarbon feedstocks from natural gas and petroleum for the purpose of producing ethylene, vinyl chloride monomer, paraffin, and industrial alcohols. These intermediary products are eithei sold to commodity customers or represent raw materials for use in further processing within the Marriott system.

3. *Hard mineral production.* Remaining activities of Marriott's business come in the exploration for and production of hard minerals. In 1973 the company opened a uranium plant in Overton, Texas, and since then has expanded its search for additional deposits in all four states. The company is presently conducting negotiations with New Mexico for obtaining the drilling rights for a potential copper deposit believed to exist north of Santa Fe. Even though Marriott is relatively new in the mineral production and research area, it is quickly becoming an area of increasing importance to the enterprise.

More recently, however, the management at Marriott, due to increasing costs and long-term commitments, has had to restrain the investment in the firm's major research projects. This recent inability to conduct the research deemed to be essential to the business has its roots in two areas. First, the company is encountering a deterioration in its working capital position. As can be seen in Exhibit 1, the current ratio in 1976 was approximately .92, while in the current year a decline to approximately .80 materialized. More specifically, the company is having difficulty in generating the cash necessary to meet the everyday working capital needs. For a case in point, the cash position (Exhibit 1) declined from $1,054,000 in 1976 to $218,000 in the present year. As a result of the working capital shortage, Marriott has felt compelled to decrease the allocation of funds being directed to research and development as well as for plant and equipment expenditures.

The second problem being encountered has been the cyclicity in corporate revenues. As can be seen in Exhibit 2, during the past five years, sales have ranged from a high of $48,293,000 in 1974 to a low of $26,674,000 in 1975. Similarly, the earnings available to common stockholders have been subject to large fluctuations. As a consequence of the uncertainty in profits, dividend payments to the common shareholders have been terminated intermittently during the past several years, including the most recent period.

Because of these circumstances, a special meeting of the board of directors was called on June 27, 1977. At the meeting John Wizard, vice-president of research and development, pressed the other board members to realize that unless the current financial trends of Marriott were reversed, the company would be lagging behind competitors in the near-term future. After a convincing presentation on the part of Wizard, the board decided to appoint David Perot, vice-president of finance, as chairman of a special committee to analyze various alternative measures for solving the financial difficulties facing Marriott. He was to report back to the board concerning his findings, with the board in turn developing a presentation for the forthcoming annual stockholder's meeting in December.

On October 23, 1977, Perot returned to the board with the committee's analysis. The committee believed that an amount between $12 million and $15 million would be required for providing sufficient capital. These funds would be employed to relieve the existing deficiency in research and development, and for solving the shortage in working capital.

The committee presented three possible avenues for raising the necessary financing:

Alternative 1.   Based upon preliminary discussions with James Monroe of Lehman Brothers concerning the issuance of common stock, Monroe noted that such an offering could feasibly be made in February 1978. This time frame was selected in view of the fact that market analysts were predicitng an upturn in the market in early 1978. Such timing should result in Marriott receiving a higher price for its stock, thus necessitating issuance of a fewer number of shares. Furthermore, Monroe believes that the underwriting would net the firm, after flotation costs, approximately $2.87 per share. If this alter-

EXHIBIT 1

Marriott Corporation

*Consolidated Balance Sheets as of
December 31, 1976 and December 31, 1977
(Dollar Figures in Thousands)*

Assets

Current Assets	1976	1977
Cash	$ 1,054	$ 218
Accounts Receivables, less allowances	5,254	5,683
Inventories, at lower of costs or market	10,521	11,211
Prepaid Expenses	312	112
Total Current Assets	17,141	17,224
Property, Plant, and Equipment		
Land	455	511
Buildings and Improvements	16,238	16,084
Machinery and Equipment	21,569	22,773
Allowances for Depreciation	(8,522)	(8,984)
Net Property, Plant, and Equipment	29,740	30,384
Other Assets	723	844
Total Assets	$47,604	$48,452

Liabilities and Stockholder's Equity

Current Liabilities		
Accounts Payable	$12,543	$13,866
Accrued Liabilities	4,595	5,854
Federal Income Taxes	1,583	1,721
Total Current Liabilities	18,721	21,441
Stockholder's Equity		
Common Stock, $1.00 per value; Authorized 25,000,000 shares; issued and outstanding 10,000,000 shares since 1965	10,000	10,000
Additional Paid-in Capital	4,325	4,325
Retained Earnings	14,558	12,686
Total Liabilities and Stockholder's Equity	$47,604	$48,452

native is selected, Perot, along with his committee, considers an issuance of 4,725,000 as being essential to raise the necessary funds. Thus, this financing plan would raise $13,560,750, thereby falling in the $12 to $15 million range of the company's estimated financial needs.

EXHIBIT 2

Marriott Corporation

Income Statements for the Years Ending
December 31, 1973-1977
(Dollar Figures in Thousands)

	1973	1974	1975	1976	1977
Net Sales	$31,365	$48,293	$26,674	$44,817	$33,542
Cost of Goods Sold	26,660	38,015	22,940	37,094	28,678
Gross Profit	4,705	10,278	3,734	7,723	4,864
Selling and Administrative expenses	2,615	4,811	1,780	3,926	3,002
Earnings before Interest and Taxes	2,095	5,467	1,954	3,797	1,862
Interest Expenses	129	217	183	211	194
Taxable Income	1,961	5,250	1,771	3,586	1,668
Federal Income Taxes	935	2,516	844	1,715	794
Earnings Available to Common Stock - holders	$ 1,026	$ 2,734	$ 927	$ 1,871	$ 874
Earnings Per Share	$ .1026	$ .2734	$ .0927	$ .1871	$ .0874
Dividends Per Share	-0-	$ .1000	-0-	$ .0800	-0-

Alternative 2.   Marriott could also issue long-term 8.5 percent debentures for providing the additional funds. In the preliminary negotiations with Lehman Brothers concerning the possibility of such an offering, the underwriters recommend a $13,500,000 issue, out of which floatation costs of $250,000 would have to be paid. A covenant providing for a sinking fund is thought to be essential in creating adequate marketability of the bond. In addition, the bonds would be issued with a 10-year maturity date of 1987. Lehman Brothers further advises a postponment in the offering until March 1978. Current estimates indicate a softening of long-term interest rates in conjunction with the anticipated rise in the stock market.

Alternative 3.   The management of Marriott Corporation has been working with Schmitt Corporation, a closely held fertilizer enterprise, concerning the feasibility of a merger between the two firms. Schmitt is a small, but well-known manufacturer and distributor of a specialized fertilizer and an all-purpose, water-soluble insecticide. The plant facilities and offices are located in Altanta, Georgia. Although the firm was incorporated in 1935, all of the common stock is still being held by the Schmitt family (Exhibit 3).

EXHIBIT 3

Schmitt Corporation Stockholder List [1]

	Numbers of Shares	Percentage of Total Number of Shares Outstanding
John A. Schmitt, Sr.	708,772	70.9
Mary M. Schmitt	170,522	17.1
Schmitt Foundation	84,614	8.5
John A. Schmitt, Jr.	23,036	2.2
John Schmitt, Jr., for Mary Jane Schmitt	13,056	1.3
Total	1,000,000	100.0

[1] No new shares have been issued since 1972.

With respect to Schmitt's products, the company's fertilizer and insect-icides are marketed under the name of Schmitt-Rite, with sales being primarily lawn and garden related. The revenues are normally distributed throughout the year on a relatively stable basis, and have been steadily increasing each year. The company retails its merchandise in the southern states, with a concentration in Mississippi, Alabama, Georgia, and Florida. The retail outlets include feed and seed stores, hardware stores, and agricultural cooperatives. In addition to the small retailers, the firm deals directly with several large farm operations. Also, the corporation has enjoyed phenomenal success in the area of research and development. Plans are being made to market a new multipurpose fertilizer in the spring of 1978.

John A. Schmitt Sr., the founder and principal shareholder, had served as president of the organization from its inception until 1968, at which time he was succeeded by John A. Schmitt, Jr. The Schmitt family has been the only management personnel, and the firm has continued to prosper under their leadership. As may be observed in Exhibit 4, the price of Schmitt's common stock has steadily increased during the past three years. Although the stock is not listed on an organized exchange, offers to purchase shares have been received by the Schmitt family on an infrequent basis.

Initial conferences with the Schmitt family have evidenced a genuine interest on their part in a potential acquisition. Both parties agree that the combination should be conducted via an exchange of common stock, with the Schmitt family receiving a specified number of Marriott shares upon the re-linquishment of their shares in the Schmitt Corporation. However, final settle-ment of the exchange ratio has not been accomplished. John Schmitt main-tains that the trade should be based upon the firms' relative earnings per share, while David Perot, in representing Marriott, contends that the market price of the respective securities would be a more equitable basis.

EXHIBIT 4

Market Price of Common Stock of Marriott
Corporation and Schmitt Corporation,
for years, 1975-78

	Marriott Corporation Market Prices (listed on NYSE)			Schmitt Corp. Market Prices[1]		
	High	Low	Year End	High	Low	Year End
1975	3.50	2.75	3.25	21.50	17.50	n/a
1976	4.25	3.50	3.75	23.00	21.00	n/a
1977	3.50	2.50	3.00	25.50	23.50	n/a

n/a = not available

[1]Estimate based upon offers made to members of the Schmitt family

EXHIBIT 5

Pro Forma Funds-Flow Statements, Years Ending
December 31, 1978-80

Sources of Funds	1978			Combined	
	Marriott	Schmitt	Combined	1979	1980
Sales	$34,218	$18,355	$52,573	$64,945	$68,554
Less: Cost of Goods Sold	29,085	14,940	44,025	53,952	55,781
Less: Selling and General Expenses	3,108	1,435	4,543	6,083	6,361
Less: Interest	208	-0-	208	211	213
Earnings Before Taxes	1,817	1,980	3,797	4,699	6,199
Less: Taxes	866	944	1,810	2,249	2,969
Add: Depreciation	433	315	748	765	780
Total Sources	$ 1,384	$ 1,351	$ 2,735	$ 3,215	$ 4,010
Uses of Funds					
Additions to Facilities	3,218	315	3,533	326	334
Sinking Fund	453	-0-	453	453	453
Increase in Noncurrent Assets	118	52	170	111	115
Common Dividends	-0-	-0-	-0-	438	438
Total Uses	3,789	367	4,156	1,328	1,340
Additions (deductions) to working Capital	($2,405)	$ 984	($1,421)	$ 1,887	$ 2,670

EXHIBIT 6

Projected Earnings Per Share for the Years 1978-1985

	1978	1979	1980	1981	1982	1983	1984	1985
Marriott	$.095	$.136	$.210	$.140	$.200	$.330	$.240	$.380
Schmitt	1.036	1.090	1.130	1.17	1.20	1.18	1.24	1.30

EXHIBIT 7
Schmitt Corporation
Balance Sheet
December 31, 1977
(Dollar Figures in Thousands)

Assets

Current Assets

Cash	$ 1,012
Accounts Receivable	1,315
Inventories	1,611
Prepaid Expenses	154
Total Current Assets	4,092

Property, Plant, and Equipment

Land	250
Buildings and Improvements	5,378
Machinery and Equipment	6,452
Allowances for Depreciation	(2,318)
Net Property, Plant, and Equipment	9,762
Total Assets	$13,854

Liabilities

Current Liabilities

Accounts Payable	$ 653
Accrued Liabilities	477
Federal Income Taxes	329
Total Current Liabilities	1,459

Stockholder's Equity

Common Stock, $10 par value, authorized 1,500,000 shares; issued and outstanding 1,500,000 shares since 1971	5,000
Retained Earnings	7,395
Total Liabilities and Stockholder's Equity	$13,854

EXHIBIT 8

Schmitt Corporation

Income Statement
For Year Ended December 31, 1977

Sales	$16,743
Cost of Goods Sold	13,709
Gross Profit	3,034
Selling and General Expenses	1,085
Earnings before Interest and Taxes	1,949
Interest Expense	-0-
Taxable Income	1,949
Federal Income Taxes	929
Earnings Available to Common Stockholders	$ 1,020
Earnings Per Share	$ 1.02
Dividends Per Share	0.0

EXHIBIT 9

Selected Petroleum Industry Ratios for 1977

Current Ratio	1.00
Quick Ratio	.80
Cash Ratio	.25
Receivable Turnover	4.00 times
Inventory Turnover[1]	2.80 times
Total Debt/Total Assets	40%
Return on Investment (Before Interest and Taxes)	7.50%
Times Interest Earned	9.50 times

[1] Based upon cost of goods sold.

QUESTIONS

1. What do you perceive to be Marriott's major problem areas?

2. If the acquisition plan is selected, what reason(s) might be given for the exchange ratio to be based upon (a) 1977 earnings per share, or (b) the average 1977 market prices?

3. Assume the final exchange ratio is negotiated between the two firms with the basis being a function of the market price. With this additional information, analyze Marriott's three alternatives for raising funds, citing the advantages and disadvantages of each plan.

Case 3

DICKENSON & GENTRY, INC.

(Term Structure of Interest Rates)

In February of 1968 the management consulting firm of Dickenson & Gentry (D & G) hired Sandy MacDonald, a recent MBA graduate from a large midwestern university. By April of that same year MacDonald was given her first major assignment, which involved an analysis of the current yield curve for inclusion in D & G's quarterly newsletter. The focal points of her yield curve analysis were to examine the expected changes of interest rates and to take a look at the yield spread between stocks and bonds.

In April of 1968 the nationwide economic outlook was somewhat uncertain, which added to the difficulty of MacDonald's task. She realized that this economic uncertainty was a result of many factors that would have to be taken into account in preparing her analysis.

During the last quarter of 1966, there was an undersirable buildup of inventories resulting from consumer caution and a subsequent slowdown in sales. This consumer caution, in large part due to rising prices and uncertainties emanating from national involvement in Vietnam, resulted in a dramatic rise in the personal savings rate. The overall effect of this rise in inventories and slowdown in spending was an economic downturn in 1967.

As the economy slowed, interest rates eventually fell; this resulted in a rise in residential construction, which proved to be the main impetence for a midyear 1967 pickup in business activity. Since then, the economy had been running on a strong upward course with interest rates rising significantly across all ranges of maturities.

In early 1968 the economy continued to be strong, but not without threats from the outside. The first of these was the Tet offensive in Vietnam, bringing on the possibility of a major escalation in the war and a subsequent rise in inflation at home. However, since President Lyndon Johnson's March 31 peace offensive speech, the possibility of a major escalation in Vietnam had fallen considerably with the subsequent start of serious peace talks. Additionally, in February 1968, the gold pool nations stopped supplying gold to the free markets, putting extreme pressure on U.S. gold reserves. Fortunately, by mid-March the pressure surrounding the gold crisis lifted, and it appeared the worst was over.

While world events continued to cloud the direction, the economy moved forward. In the first quarter of 1968, GNP rose by 2.5 percent or $20 billion. Of this rise, 1½ percent represents an increase in real output with the remainder representing inflationary effects. This welcome increase in real GNP was largely a result of a $16 billion increase in consumer spending, with much of this increase in consumer spending resulting from a retroactive pay raise in December, followed by an increase in social security benefits in March.

During this period there had been considerable upward pressure on interest rates. The three-month treasury bill rate rose to over 5½ percent, while the legal ceiling on large negotiable certificates of deposit was raised 3/4 of a percent to 6¼ percent. By April the prime rate had risen to 6½ percent under strong borrowing pressure, and many economists on Wall Street felt that they might rise ¼ to ½ percent more before peaking out and returning to more normal levels.

Within this economic setting, Sandy MacDonald was to analyze the current interest rate structure. In formulating the yield curve, she decided to examine U.S. government securities since they were the most common debt securities traded; hence, a wealth of information was available on them. From the most recent *Federal Reserve Bulletin,* the yields on the government securities are shown in Exhibit 1. In addition, at that time the yield on common stocks was 3.1 percent.

MacDonald's report was to involve two sections: the first, a report on the direction and magnitude of expected changes in the interest rate as revealed in the current yield curve; the second, an examination and analysis of the yield spread between stocks and bonds (see Exhibit 2).

QUESTIONS

1. Graph the yield curve for April 1968.
2. What does the shape of the yield curve tell you about investors' expectations with respect to future interest rates?
3. MacDonald also noticed that bonds selling at a discount because of a low

EXHIBIT 1

Market Quotations on Treasury Securities

Maturity Date	Market Yield
5/16/68	5.65
5/31/68	5.65
6/6/68	5.62
6/20/68	5.50
7/5/68	5.48
7/18/68	5.50
8/15/68	5.85
11/15/68	5.91
2/15/69	6.00
5/15/69	6.00
10/1/69	5.79
2/15/70	5.77
11/15/70	5.92
2/15/71	6.00
5/15/71	5.98
8/15/71	5.77
11/5/71	5.97
12/15/71	5.76
2/15/72	6.01
3/15/72	5.81
5/15/72	6.00
8/15/72	5.80
8/15/73	5.81
11/15/73	5.84
2/15/74	5.81
5/15/74	5.85
11/15/74	5.73
12/15/74	5.87
2/15/75	5.89
2/15/80	5.69
11/15/80	5.55
5/15/83	5.53
5/15/85	5.38
8/15/85	5.61
2/15/90	5.30
8/15/92	5.49
2/15/93	5.42
5/15/94	5.47
2/15/95	4.50
11/15/98	4.98

EXHIBIT 2

Stock and Bond Yields

D & G also calculates an index of stock and bond yields. This is given below for the last 10 years.

	65_4	66_1	66_2	66_3	66_4	67_1	67_2	67_3	67_4	68_1
Bond yield	4.6	4.9	5.1	5.4	5.8	5.8	5.5	5.9	6.2	6.5
Stock yield	3.1	3.3	3.4	3.5	3.3	3.2	3.1	3.0	3.1	3.1

coupon yield tended to have lower yields to maturity than similar bonds not selling at a discount (indicating that investors were willing to accept a lower yield to maturity on these bonds than similar bonds not selling at a discount). Why was this so? (Hint: Examine the tax implications of this situation.)

4. MacDonald was also directed to examine corporate bond and stock yields in an attempt to measure expected return and risk. Is this an appropriate procedure?

5. What actually happened to interest rates? Is this what investors expected? What would have happened to investors who bought long-term bonds?

6. Graph the current yield curve. What does the shape of this curve tell you about investors' expectations as to the future course of interest rates?

APPENDIX A

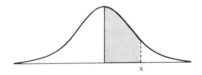

The area indicated in the table is equal to the area between the mean and x standard deviations to the right or left of the mean.

Number of Standard Deviations from the Mean (x)	Area	Number of Standard Deviations from the Mean (x)	Area
.00	.00000	.12	.04776
.01	.00399	.13	.05172
.02	.00798	.14	.05567
.03	.01197	.15	.05962
.04	.01595	.16	.06356
.05	.01994	.17	.06749
.06	.02392	.18	.07142
.07	.02790	.19	.07535
.08	.03188	.20	.07926
.09	.03586	.21	.08317
.10	.03983	.22	.08706
.11	.04380	.23	.09095

Number of Standard Deviations from the Mean (x)	Area	Number of Standard Deviations from the Mean (x)	Area
.24	.09483	.67	.24857
.25	.09871	.68	.25175
.26	.10257	.69	.25490
.27	.10642	.70	.25804
.28	.11026	.71	.26115
.29	.11409	.72	.26424
.30	.11791	.73	.26730
.31	.12172	.74	.27035
.32	.12552	.75	.27337
.33	.12930	.76	.27637
.34	.13307	.77	.27935
.35	.13683	.78	.28230
.36	.14058	.79	.28524
.37	.14431	.80	.28814
.38	.14803	.81	.29103
.39	.15173	.82	.29389
.40	.15542	.83	.29673
.41	.15910	.84	.29955
.42	.16276	.85	.30234
.43	.16640	.86	.30511
.44	.17003	.87	.30785
.45	.17364	.88	.31057
.46	.17724	.89	.31327
.47	.18082	.90	.31594
.48	.18439	.91	.31859
.49	.18793	.92	.32121
.50	.19146	.93	.32381
.51	.19497	.94	.32639
.52	.19847	.95	.32894
.53	.20194	.96	.33147
.54	.20540	.97	.33398
.55	.20884	.98	.33646
.56	.21226	.99	.33891
.57	.21566	1.00	.34134
.58	.21904	1.01	.34375
.59	.22240	1.02	.34614
.60	.22575	1.03	.34849
.61	.22907	1.04	.35083
.62	.23237	1.05	.35314
.63	.23565	1.06	.35543
.64	.23891	1.07	.35769
.65	.24215	1.08	.35993
.66	.24537	1.09	.36214

Number of Standard Deviations from the Mean (x)	Area	Number of Standard Deviations from the Mean (x)	Area
1.10	.36433	1.53	.43699
1.11	.36650	1.54	.43822
1.12	.36864	1.55	.43943
1.13	.37076	1.56	.44062
1.14	.37286	1.57	.44179
1.15	.37493	1.58	.44295
1.16	.37698	1.59	.44408
1.17	.37900	1.60	.44520
1.18	.38100	1.61	.44630
1.19	.38298	1.62	.44738
1.20	.38493	1.63	.44845
1.21	.38686	1.64	.44950
1.22	.38877	1.65	.45053
1.23	.39065	1.66	.45154
1.24	.39251	1.67	.45254
1.25	.39435	1.68	.45352
1.26	.39617	1.69	.45449
1.27	.39796	1.70	.45543
1.28	.39973	1.71	.45637
1.29	.40147	1.72	.45728
1.30	.40320	1.73	.45818
1.31	.40490	1.74	.45907
1.32	.40658	1.75	.45994
1.33	.40824	1.76	.46080
1.34	.40988	1.77	.46164
1.35	.41149	1.78	.46246
1.36	.41309	1.79	.46327
1.37	.41466	1.80	.46407
1.38	.41621	1.81	.46485
1.39	.41774	1.82	.46562
1.40	.41924	1.83	.46638
1.41	.42073	1.84	.46712
1.42	.42220	1.85	.46784
1.43	.42364	1.86	.46856
1.44	.42507	1.87	.46926
1.45	.42647	1.88	.46995
1.46	.42785	1.89	.47062
1.47	.42922	1.90	.47128
1.48	.43056	1.91	.47193
1.49	.43189	1.92	.47257
1.50	.43319	1.93	.47320
1.51	.43448	1.94	.47381
1.52	.43574	1.95	.47441

Number of Standard Deviations from the Mean (x)	Area	Number of Standard Deviations from the Mean (x)	Area
1.96	.47500	2.39	.49158
1.97	.47558	2.40	.49180
1.98	.47615	2.41	.49202
1.99	.47670	2.42	.49224
2.00	.47725	2.43	.49245
2.01	.47778	2.44	.49266
2.02	.47831	2.45	.49286
2.03	.47882	2.46	.49305
2.04	.47932	2.47	.49324
2.05	.47982	2.48	.49343
2.06	.48030	2.49	.49361
2.07	.48077	2.50	.49379
2.08	.48124	2.51	.49396
2.09	.48169	2.52	.49413
2.10	.48214	2.53	.49430
2.11	.48257	2.54	.49446
2.12	.48300	2.55	.49461
2.13	.48341	2.56	.49477
2.14	.48382	2.57	.49492
2.15	.48422	2.58	.49506
2.16	.48461	2.59	.49520
2.17	.48500	2.60	.49534
2.18	.48537	2.61	.49547
2.19	.48574	2.62	.49560
2.20	.48610	2.63	.49573
2.21	.48645	2.64	.49585
2.22	.48679	2.65	.49598
2.23	.48713	2.66	.49609
2.24	.48745	2.67	.49621
2.25	.48778	2.68	.49632
2.26	.48809	2.69	.49643
2.27	.48840	2.70	.49653
2.28	.48870	2.71	.49664
2.29	.48899	2.72	.49674
2.30	.48928	2.73	.49683
2.31	.48956	2.74	.49693
2.32	.48983	2.75	.49702
2.33	.49010	2.76	.49711
2.34	.49036	2.77	.49720
2.35	.49061	2.78	.49728
2.36	.49086	2.79	.49736
2.37	.49111	2.80	.49744
2.38	.49134	2.81	.49752

Number of Standard Deviations from the Mean (x)	Area	Number of Standard Deviations from the Mean (x)	Area
2.82	.49760	3.25	.49942
2.83	.49767	3.26	.49944
2.84	.49774	3.27	.49946
2.85	.49781	3.28	.49948
2.86	.49788	3.29	.49950
2.87	.49795	3.30	.49952
2.88	.49801	3.31	.49953
2.89	.49807	3.32	.49955
2.90	.49813	3.33	.49957
2.91	.49819	3.34	.49958
2.92	.49825	3.35	.49960
2.93	.49831	3.36	.49961
2.94	.49836	3.37	.49962
2.95	.49841	3.38	.49964
2.96	.49846	3.39	.49965
2.97	.49851	3.40	.49966
2.98	.49856	3.41	.49968
2.99	.49861	3.42	.49969
3.00	.49865	3.43	.49970
3.01	.49869	3.44	.49971
3.02	.49874	3.45	.49972
3.03	.49878	3.46	.49973
3.04	.49882	3.47	.49974
3.05	.49886	3.48	.49975
3.06	.49889	3.49	.49976
3.07	.49893	3.50	.49977
3.08	.49896	3.51	.49978
3.09	.49900	3.52	.49978
3.10	.49903	3.53	.49979
3.11	.49906	3.54	.49980
3.12	.49910	3.55	.49981
3.13	.49913	3.56	.49981
3.14	.49916	3.57	.49982
3.15	.49918	3.58	.49983
3.16	.49921	3.59	.49983
3.17	.49924	3.60	.49984
3.18	.49926	3.61	.49985
3.19	.49929	3.62	.49985
3.20	.49931	3.63	.49986
3.21	.49934	3.64	.49986
3.22	.49936	3.65	.49987
3.23	.49938	3.66	.49987
3.24	.49940	3.67	.49988

Number of Standard Deviations from the Mean (x)	Area	Number of Standard Deviations from the Mean (x)	Area
3.68	.49988	3.84	.49994
3.69	.49989	3.85	.49994
3.70	.49989	3.86	.49994
3.71	.49990	3.87	.49995
3.72	.49990	3.88	.49995
3.73	.49990	3.89	.49995
3.74	.49991	3.90	.49995
3.75	.49991	3.91	.49995
3.76	.49992	3.92	.49996
3.77	.49992	3.93	.49996
3.78	.49992	3.94	.49996
3.79	.49992	3.95	.49996
3.80	.49993	3.96	.49996
3.81	.49993	3.97	.49996
3.82	.49993	3.98	.49997
3.83	.49994	3.99	.49997

Source: This table is condensed and derived from *Tables of Normal Probability Functions*, National Bureau of Standards, Applied Mathematics Series 23 (Washington, D.C.; U.S. Government Printing Office; 1953).

APPENDIX B

TABLE A1 -- COMPOUND SUM OF $1 FOR N YEARS

INTEREST RATES

N	0.01	0.02	0.03	0.04	0.05	0.06	0.07	0.08	0.09	0.10
1	1.01000	1.02000	1.03000	1.04000	1.05000	1.06000	1.07000	1.08000	1.09000	1.10000
2	1.02010	1.04040	1.06090	1.08160	1.10250	1.12360	1.14490	1.16640	1.18810	1.21000
3	1.03030	1.06121	1.09272	1.12486	1.15762	1.19101	1.22504	1.25971	1.29502	1.33100
4	1.04060	1.08243	1.12551	1.16986	1.21550	1.26247	1.31079	1.36049	1.41158	1.46410
5	1.05101	1.10408	1.15927	1.21665	1.27628	1.33822	1.40255	1.46932	1.53862	1.61051
6	1.06152	1.12616	1.19405	1.26532	1.34009	1.41851	1.50072	1.58687	1.67709	1.77155
7	1.07213	1.14868	1.22987	1.31593	1.40709	1.50362	1.60577	1.71382	1.82803	1.94870
8	1.08285	1.17165	1.26676	1.36856	1.47744	1.59384	1.71817	1.85092	1.99255	2.14357
9	1.09367	1.19508	1.30476	1.42330	1.55131	1.68946	1.83845	1.99899	2.17187	2.35793
10	1.10461	1.21898	1.34391	1.48024	1.62888	1.79084	1.96714	2.15891	2.36734	2.59372
11	1.11565	1.24336	1.38422	1.53944	1.71032	1.89828	2.10483	2.33162	2.58040	2.85309
12	1.12681	1.26823	1.42575	1.60102	1.79583	2.01217	2.25217	2.51815	2.81263	3.13840
13	1.13807	1.29359	1.46852	1.66506	1.88562	2.13290	2.40982	2.71960	3.06576	3.45223
14	1.14945	1.31946	1.51257	1.73166	1.97990	2.26087	2.57850	2.93717	3.34168	3.79745
15	1.16095	1.34585	1.55795	1.80093	2.07890	2.39652	2.75900	3.17214	3.64243	4.17719
16	1.17255	1.37277	1.60468	1.87296	2.18284	2.54031	2.95212	3.42591	3.97024	4.59491
17	1.18428	1.40022	1.65282	1.94788	2.29198	2.69273	3.15877	3.69998	4.32756	5.05440
18	1.19612	1.42822	1.70241	2.02579	2.40658	2.85429	3.37988	3.99598	4.71704	5.55983
19	1.20808	1.45679	1.75348	2.10683	2.52690	3.02555	3.61647	4.31565	5.14156	6.11581
20	1.22016	1.48592	1.80608	2.19110	2.65324	3.20707	3.86962	4.66090	5.60430	6.72738
21	1.23236	1.51564	1.86026	2.27874	2.78590	3.39950	4.14049	5.03377	6.10868	7.40011
22	1.24468	1.54595	1.91607	2.36989	2.92520	3.60346	4.43032	5.43647	6.65846	8.14012
23	1.25712	1.57687	1.97355	2.46468	3.07145	3.81967	4.74044	5.87138	7.25771	8.95412
24	1.26969	1.60841	2.03275	2.56327	3.22502	4.04884	5.07227	6.34109	7.91090	9.84952
25	1.28239	1.64057	2.09373	2.66580	3.38627	4.29177	5.42732	6.84838	8.62287	10.83447
26	1.29521	1.67338	2.15654	2.77243	3.55558	4.54927	5.80723	7.39624	9.39892	11.91790
27	1.30816	1.70685	2.22124	2.88332	3.73335	4.82222	6.21373	7.98794	10.24481	13.10968
28	1.32124	1.74098	2.28787	2.99865	3.92002	5.11155	6.64868	8.62696	11.16683	14.42064
29	1.33445	1.77580	2.35651	3.11860	4.11602	5.41824	7.11409	9.31712	12.17183	15.86269
30	1.34780	1.81132	2.42720	3.24334	4.32181	5.74332	7.61206	10.06248	13.26729	17.44893

TABLE A1 -- COMPOUND SUM OF $1 FOR N YEARS

INTEREST RATES

N	0.11	0.12	0.13	0.14	0.15	0.16	0.17	0.18	0.19	0.20
1	1.11000	1.12000	1.13000	1.14000	1.15000	1.16000	1.17000	1.18000	1.19000	1.20000
2	1.23210	1.25440	1.27690	1.29960	1.32250	1.34560	1.36890	1.39240	1.41610	1.44000
3	1.36763	1.40493	1.44289	1.48154	1.52087	1.56089	1.60161	1.64303	1.68516	1.72800
4	1.51807	1.57352	1.63047	1.68896	1.74900	1.81064	1.87388	1.93877	2.00533	2.07360
5	1.68505	1.76234	1.84243	1.92541	2.01135	2.10034	2.19244	2.28775	2.38635	2.48831
6	1.87041	1.97382	2.08194	2.19496	2.31305	2.43639	2.56515	2.69955	2.83975	2.98598
7	2.07615	2.21067	2.35259	2.50225	2.66001	2.82621	3.00122	3.18546	3.37931	3.58317
8	2.30453	2.47596	2.65842	2.85256	3.05901	3.27840	3.51142	3.75883	4.02137	4.29980
9	2.55802	2.77307	3.00401	3.25192	3.51785	3.80295	4.10836	4.43542	4.78542	5.15976
10	2.83940	3.10584	3.39453	3.70718	4.04553	4.41142	4.80678	5.23379	5.69463	6.19171
11	3.15173	3.47853	3.83531	4.22618	4.65236	5.11724	5.62393	6.17587	6.77663	7.43004
12	3.49842	3.89596	4.33447	4.81785	5.35021	5.93600	6.57998	7.28752	8.06416	8.91605
13	3.88325	4.36347	4.89794	5.49234	6.15273	6.88576	7.69958	8.59927	9.59638	10.69925
14	4.31040	4.88708	5.53467	6.26126	7.07564	7.98747	9.00732	10.14712	11.41968	12.83910
15	4.78454	5.47353	6.25416	7.13783	8.13698	9.26546	10.53856	11.97360	13.58941	15.40591
16	5.31084	6.13035	7.06720	8.13711	9.35752	10.74793	12.33013	14.12883	16.17139	18.48827
17	5.89503	6.86991	7.98593	9.27631	10.76114	12.46760	14.42623	16.67201	19.24394	22.18591
18	6.54347	7.68991	9.02409	10.57498	12.37530	14.46241	16.87363	19.67294	22.90027	26.62308
19	7.26325	8.61269	10.19721	12.05546	14.23158	16.77638	19.74799	23.21407	27.25130	31.94768
20	8.06220	9.64621	11.52283	13.74321	16.36630	19.46059	23.10510	27.39256	32.42903	38.33719
21	8.94904	10.80376	13.02079	15.66724	18.82124	22.57428	27.03296	32.32320	38.59053	46.00461
22	9.93343	12.10020	14.71347	17.86663	21.64441	26.18616	31.62852	38.14134	45.92271	55.20549
23	11.02609	13.55221	16.62619	20.36110	24.89105	30.37592	37.00534	45.00676	54.64798	66.24657
24	12.23896	15.17848	18.78758	23.21162	28.62468	35.23607	43.29619	53.10793	65.03107	79.49533
25	13.58523	16.99988	21.22995	26.46124	32.91837	40.87383	50.65649	62.66731	77.38693	95.39497
26	15.07960	19.03986	23.98982	30.16577	37.85609	47.41362	59.26805	73.94736	92.05041	114.47389
27	16.73833	21.32463	27.10846	34.38895	43.53448	54.99976	69.34354	87.25783	109.58749	137.36862
28	18.57954	23.88358	30.63252	39.20355	50.06462	63.79970	81.13185	102.96411	130.40907	164.84224
29	20.62328	26.74960	34.61472	44.69460	57.57428	74.00764	94.92419	121.49756	155.18671	197.81067
30	22.89183	29.95955	39.11458	50.94858	66.21037	85.84883	111.06117	143.36697	184.67207	237.37262

TABLE A1 -- COMPOUND SUM OF $1 FOR N YEARS

INTEREST RATES

N	0.21	0.22	0.23	0.24	0.25	0.26	0.27	0.28	0.29	0.30
1	1.21000	1.22000	1.23000	1.24000	1.25000	1.26000	1.27000	1.28000	1.29000	1.33000
2	1.46410	1.48840	1.51290	1.53760	1.56250	1.58760	1.61290	1.63840	1.56410	1.69000
3	1.77156	1.81584	1.86086	1.90662	1.95313	2.00037	2.04838	2.09715	2.14669	2.19699
4	2.14358	2.21533	2.28886	2.36421	2.44141	2.52047	2.60144	2.68435	2.76923	2.85609
5	2.59373	2.70270	2.81530	2.93162	3.05176	3.17579	3.30383	3.43597	3.57230	3.71292
6	3.13841	3.29729	3.46281	3.63520	3.81470	4.00149	4.19536	4.39804	4.60827	4.82679
7	3.79747	4.02269	4.25926	4.50765	4.76837	5.04187	5.32873	5.62949	5.94467	6.27482
8	4.59493	4.90767	5.23889	5.59948	5.96046	6.35275	6.76749	7.20574	7.66862	8.15726
9	5.55986	5.98736	6.44483	6.93096	7.45058	8.00446	8.59470	9.22334	9.89252	10.60443
10	6.72743	7.30457	7.92590	8.59438	9.31323	10.08562	10.91526	11.80588	12.76134	13.78575
11	8.14018	8.91157	9.74885	10.65703	11.64153	12.70787	13.86238	15.11152	16.46213	17.92145
12	9.84960	10.87211	11.99108	13.21471	14.55192	16.01190	17.60519	19.34273	21.23613	23.29787
13	11.91801	13.26396	14.74903	16.38623	18.18988	20.17497	22.35860	24.75868	27.39461	30.28722
14	14.42077	16.18201	18.14128	20.31891	22.73737	25.42044	28.39539	31.69112	35.33905	39.37335
15	17.44911	19.74203	22.31377	25.19543	28.42171	32.02974	36.06212	40.56461	45.58737	51.18530
16	21.11340	24.08527	27.44592	31.24232	35.52713	40.35745	45.79887	51.92268	58.80769	66.54085
17	25.54723	29.38400	33.75847	38.74046	44.40891	50.85036	58.16454	66.46101	75.86191	86.50304
18	30.91206	35.84845	41.52289	48.03815	55.51114	64.07140	73.86890	85.07007	97.86186	112.45387
19	37.40356	43.73536	51.07312	59.56726	69.38892	80.72990	93.81345	108.88963	126.24179	146.18988
20	45.25826	53.35674	62.81990	73.86339	86.73615	101.71960	119.14299	139.37869	162.85185	190.04674
21	54.76244	65.09517	77.26845	91.59058	108.42020	128.16663	151.31152	178.40469	210.07883	247.06059
22	66.26247	79.41623	95.04013	113.57222	135.52524	161.48981	192.16548	228.35793	271.00171	321.17847
23	80.17751	96.88748	116.89926	140.82947	169.40656	203.47702	244.04999	292.29785	349.59204	417.53149
24	97.01466	118.20265	143.78606	174.62848	211.75819	256.38086	309.94312	374.14136	450.97363	542.79077
25	117.38765	144.20712	176.85677	216.53926	264.69751	323.03955	393.62769	478.90063	581.75610	705.62744
26	142.03886	175.93253	217.53368	268.50830	330.87207	407.02954	499.90674	612.99268	750.46509	917.31519
27	171.96688	214.63751	267.56616	332.95020	413.59009	512.85693	634.88110	784.63037	968.09961	1192.50830
28	207.95863	261.85742	329.10620	412.85815	516.98755	646.19946	806.27893	1004.32617	1248.84766	1550.25977
29	251.62975	319.46582	404.80054	511.94385	646.23413	814.21045	1023.99854	1285.53711	1611.01367	2015.33691
30	304.47144	389.74780	497.90405	634.80981	807.79321	1025.90405	1300.47656	1645.48779	2078.20801	2619.93604

208

TABLE A2 -- COMPOUND AMOUNT OF AN N YEAR ANNUITY

INTEREST RATES

N	0.01	0.02	0.03	0.04	0.05	0.06	0.07	0.08	0.09	0.10
1	1.00000	1.00000	1.00000	1.00000	1.00000	1.00000	1.00000	1.00000	1.00000	1.00000
2	2.01000	2.02000	2.03000	2.04000	2.05000	2.06000	2.07000	2.08000	2.09000	2.10000
3	3.03010	3.06040	3.09090	3.12160	3.15250	3.18360	3.21490	3.24640	3.27810	3.31000
4	4.06039	4.12160	4.18362	4.24646	4.31012	4.37461	4.43994	4.50611	4.57312	4.64099
5	5.10099	5.20403	5.30913	5.41632	5.52562	5.63708	5.75073	5.86660	5.98470	6.10509
6	6.15200	6.30811	6.46840	6.63297	6.80190	6.97530	7.15328	7.33592	7.52331	7.71559
7	7.21351	7.43427	7.66245	7.89828	8.14198	8.39381	8.65400	8.92279	9.20041	9.48714
8	8.28563	8.58295	8.89231	9.21421	9.54907	9.89743	10.25977	10.63661	11.02843	11.43585
9	9.36848	9.75460	10.15907	10.58277	11.02652	11.49127	11.97795	12.48753	13.02098	13.57942
10	10.46215	10.94968	11.46384	12.00608	12.57783	13.18073	13.81639	14.48652	15.19285	15.93735
11	11.56676	12.16867	12.80774	13.48631	14.20671	14.97157	15.78353	16.64543	17.56018	18.53107
12	12.68241	13.41203	14.19197	15.02576	15.91703	16.86984	17.88835	18.97705	20.14056	21.38416
13	13.80922	14.68026	15.61771	16.62677	17.71286	18.88200	20.14052	21.49519	22.95319	24.52254
14	14.94729	15.97385	17.08623	18.29184	19.59848	21.01489	22.55034	24.21478	26.01894	27.97476
15	16.09674	17.29330	18.59879	20.02350	21.57838	23.27576	25.12883	27.15189	29.36061	31.77220
16	17.25769	18.63914	20.15672	21.82442	23.65727	25.67227	27.88782	30.32408	33.00304	35.94939
17	18.43024	20.01190	21.76140	23.69737	25.84010	28.21257	30.83994	33.74998	36.97327	40.54428
18	19.61450	21.41211	23.41461	25.64537	28.13208	30.90529	33.99870	37.44998	41.30083	45.59866
19	20.81061	22.84033	25.11662	27.67104	30.53865	33.75957	37.37857	41.44594	46.01785	51.15849
20	22.01868	24.29712	26.87009	29.77785	33.06555	36.78511	40.99504	45.76158	51.15941	57.27429
21	23.23883	25.78304	28.67648	31.96893	35.71888	39.99229	44.86465	50.42247	56.76408	64.00166
22	24.47118	27.29866	30.53642	34.24767	38.50470	43.39229	49.00514	55.45624	62.87238	71.40176
23	25.71585	28.84460	32.45248	36.61754	41.42989	46.99592	53.43546	60.89270	69.53082	79.54187
24	26.97296	30.42146	34.42603	39.08221	44.50133	50.81477	58.17589	66.76408	76.78853	88.49599
25	28.24265	32.02986	36.45877	41.64548	47.72635	54.86360	63.24815	73.10516	84.69942	98.34550
26	29.52502	33.67043	38.55249	44.31126	51.11261	59.15536	68.67548	79.95354	93.32228	109.17996
27	30.82024	35.34380	40.70903	47.08368	54.66818	63.70838	74.48270	87.34978	102.72119	121.09785
28	32.12839	37.05064	42.93027	49.96700	58.40154	68.52684	80.69643	95.33771	112.96599	134.20752
29	33.44962	38.79163	45.21814	52.96564	62.32155	73.63838	87.34511	103.96466	124.13281	148.62814
30	34.78406	40.56741	47.57465	56.08423	66.43756	79.05661	94.45920	113.28177	136.30464	164.49083

TABLE A2 -- COMPOUND AMOUNT OF AN N YEAR ANNUITY

INTEREST RATES

N	0.11	0.12	0.13	0.14	0.15	0.16	0.17	0.18	0.19	0.20
1	1.00000	1.00000	1.00000	1.00000	1.00000	1.00000	1.00000	1.00000	1.00000	1.00000
2	2.11000	2.12000	2.13000	2.14000	2.15000	2.16000	2.17000	2.18000	2.19000	2.20000
3	3.34210	3.37440	3.40690	3.43960	3.47250	3.50560	3.53890	3.57240	3.60610	3.64000
4	4.70973	4.77933	4.84690	4.92114	4.99337	5.06649	5.14050	5.21543	5.29125	5.36800
5	6.22779	6.35284	6.48026	6.61009	6.74237	6.87713	7.01438	7.15420	7.29659	7.44159
6	7.91285	8.11518	8.32268	8.53550	8.75372	8.97747	9.20682	9.44195	9.68294	9.92991
7	9.78325	10.08900	10.40462	10.73046	11.06681	11.41386	11.77197	12.14149	12.52269	12.91588
8	11.85940	12.29967	12.75721	13.23271	13.72678	14.24007	14.77319	15.32694	15.90199	16.49904
9	14.16393	14.77563	15.41563	16.08527	16.78578	17.51846	18.28461	19.08577	19.92336	20.79884
10	16.72194	17.54869	18.41963	19.33719	20.30363	21.32141	22.39296	23.52118	24.70877	25.95859
11	19.56134	20.65453	21.81415	23.04437	24.34915	25.73282	27.19974	28.75496	30.40341	32.15028
12	22.71307	24.13306	25.64995	27.27055	29.00150	30.85035	32.82365	34.93082	37.18004	39.58032
13	26.21149	28.02901	29.98441	32.08839	34.35170	36.78604	39.40363	42.21832	45.24422	48.49637
14	30.09473	32.39247	34.88234	37.58073	40.50443	43.67178	47.10219	50.81758	54.84059	59.19562
15	34.40512	37.27954	40.41699	43.84198	47.58005	51.65926	56.10950	60.96469	66.26027	72.03471
16	39.18965	42.75307	46.67114	50.97980	55.71701	60.92471	66.64804	72.93828	79.84967	87.44162
17	44.50049	48.88341	53.73834	59.11690	65.07452	71.67264	78.97813	87.06711	96.02106	105.92989
18	50.39551	55.74939	61.72426	68.39319	75.83566	84.14023	93.40433	103.73912	115.26500	128.11580
19	56.93898	63.43929	70.74834	78.96815	88.21195	98.60263	110.28296	123.41206	138.16527	154.73888
20	64.20222	72.05197	80.94554	91.02361	102.44254	115.37901	130.03094	146.62613	165.41656	186.68655
21	72.26442	81.69818	92.46837	104.76680	118.80884	134.83960	153.13605	174.01869	197.84760	225.02374
22	81.21346	92.50194	105.48915	120.43604	137.63008	157.41388	180.16901	206.34189	236.43613	271.02832
23	91.14688	104.60215	120.20261	138.29466	159.27649	183.60104	211.79753	244.48323	282.35864	326.23364
24	102.17297	118.15433	136.82880	158.65576	184.16554	213.97595	248.80287	289.49499	337.00659	392.47998
25	114.41193	133.33279	155.61638	181.86739	212.79022	249.21202	292.09888	342.59790	402.33760	471.97559
26	127.99715	150.33267	176.84633	208.32863	245.70859	290.08569	342.75537	405.26514	479.42432	567.37036
27	143.07674	169.37253	200.83615	238.49940	283.56445	337.49927	402.02319	479.22140	571.51465	681.84424
28	159.81506	190.69716	227.94461	272.88930	327.10388	392.49902	471.63670	566.47021	681.10205	819.21265
29	178.39461	214.58073	258.57690	312.08643	377.16933	456.29858	552.49854	669.43433	811.51099	984.05469
30	199.01788	241.33034	293.19141	356.77808	434.73755	530.30615	647.42261	790.93188	966.69751	1181.86523

INTEREST RATES

N	0.21	0.22	0.23	0.24	0.25	0.26	0.27	0.28	0.29	0.30
1	1.00000	1.00000	1.00000	1.00000	1.00000	1.00000	1.00000	1.00000	1.00000	1.00000
2	2.21000	2.22000	2.23000	2.24000	2.25000	2.26000	2.27000	2.28000	2.29000	2.30000
3	3.67410	3.70840	3.74290	3.77760	3.81250	3.84760	3.88290	3.91840	3.95410	3.99000
4	5.44565	5.52424	5.60376	5.68422	5.76563	5.84797	5.93128	6.01555	6.10079	6.18699
5	7.58923	7.73957	7.89262	8.04843	8.20703	8.36844	8.53272	8.69990	8.87002	9.04308
6	10.18296	10.44226	10.70792	10.98005	11.25879	11.54422	11.83654	12.13587	12.44232	12.75600
7	13.32137	13.73955	14.17074	14.61525	15.07349	15.54571	16.03239	16.53391	17.05058	17.58278
8	17.11884	17.76224	18.42999	19.12289	19.84186	20.58757	21.36113	22.16339	22.99524	23.85759
9	21.71376	22.66991	23.66887	24.71237	25.80232	26.94032	28.12862	29.36913	30.66385	32.01485
10	27.27362	28.65725	30.11269	31.64333	33.25290	34.94478	36.72331	38.59247	40.55637	42.61926
11	34.00104	35.96182	38.03857	40.23770	42.56612	45.03038	47.63857	50.39835	53.31770	56.40503
12	42.14120	44.87338	47.78741	50.89471	54.20764	57.73824	61.52093	65.50986	69.77983	74.32645
13	51.99080	55.74548	59.77849	64.10942	68.75955	73.75014	79.10612	84.85258	91.01596	97.62431
14	63.90880	69.00943	74.52751	80.49565	86.94943	93.92511	101.46472	109.61127	118.41057	127.91153
15	78.32956	85.19144	92.66879	100.81456	109.68680	119.34555	129.86011	141.30238	153.74962	167.28488
16	95.77867	104.93347	114.98256	126.00999	138.10851	151.37529	165.92223	181.86699	199.33699	218.47018
17	116.89207	129.01874	142.42848	157.25232	173.63564	191.73274	211.72110	233.78967	258.14453	295.01099
18	142.43927	158.40274	176.18695	195.99278	218.04454	242.58310	269.88550	300.25049	334.06635	371.51392
19	173.35133	194.25119	217.70984	244.03093	273.55566	306.65430	343.75439	385.32056	431.86816	483.96777
20	210.75490	237.98625	268.78296	303.59814	342.94458	387.38403	437.56763	494.20996	558.10986	630.15747
21	256.01294	291.34277	331.60278	377.46143	429.68066	489.10352	556.71045	633.58862	720.96167	820.20410
22	310.77539	356.43774	408.87109	469.05200	538.10083	617.27002	708.02197	811.99316	931.04028	1067.26465
23	377.03784	435.85376	503.91113	582.62402	673.62598	778.75977	900.18726	1040.35107	1202.04199	1388.44312
24	457.21533	532.74121	620.81030	723.45337	843.03247	982.23657	1144.23706	1332.64893	1551.63403	1805.97461
25	554.22998	650.94385	764.59619	898.08179	1054.79053	1238.61743	1454.18018	1706.79028	2002.60767	2348.76538
26	671.61743	795.15088	941.45288	1114.62085	1319.48804	1561.65698	1847.80786	2185.69092	2584.36377	3054.39282
27	813.65625	971.08325	1158.98633	1383.12915	1650.36011	1968.68652	2347.71460	2798.68359	3334.82886	3971.70801
28	985.52295	1185.72070	1426.55249	1716.07935	2063.95020	2481.54346	2982.90775	3583.31396	4302.92576	5164.21484
29	1193.48145	1447.57813	1755.65869	2128.93750	2580.93774	3127.74292	3788.89355	4587.63672	5551.77344	6714.47266
30	1445.11108	1767.04395	2160.45923	2640.88135	3227.17188	3941.95337	4812.89063	5873.17188	7162.78516	8729.83859

TABLE B1 -- PRESENT VALUE OF $1 DUE AT THE END OF N YEARS

INTEREST RATES

N	0.01	0.02	0.03	0.04	0.05	0.06	0.07	0.08	0.09	0.10
1	0.99010	0.98039	0.97087	0.96154	0.95238	0.94340	0.93458	0.92593	0.91743	0.90909
2	0.98030	0.96117	0.94260	0.92456	0.90703	0.89000	0.87344	0.85734	0.84168	0.82645
3	0.97059	0.94232	0.91514	0.88900	0.86384	0.83962	0.81630	0.79383	0.77219	0.75132
4	0.96099	0.92385	0.88849	0.85481	0.82271	0.79210	0.76290	0.73503	0.70843	0.68302
5	0.95147	0.90573	0.86261	0.82193	0.78353	0.74726	0.71299	0.68059	0.64993	0.62092
6	0.94205	0.88798	0.83749	0.79032	0.74622	0.70496	0.66635	0.63017	0.59627	0.56448
7	0.93273	0.87056	0.81310	0.75992	0.71069	0.66506	0.62275	0.58349	0.54704	0.51316
8	0.92349	0.85350	0.78941	0.73069	0.67684	0.62742	0.58201	0.54027	0.50187	0.46651
9	0.91435	0.83676	0.76642	0.70259	0.64461	0.59190	0.54394	0.50025	0.46043	0.42410
10	0.90530	0.82035	0.74410	0.67557	0.61392	0.55840	0.50835	0.46320	0.42241	0.38555
11	0.89634	0.80427	0.72243	0.64958	0.58469	0.52679	0.47510	0.42889	0.38754	0.35050
12	0.88746	0.78850	0.70139	0.62460	0.55684	0.49693	0.44402	0.39712	0.35554	0.31863
13	0.87868	0.77304	0.68096	0.60058	0.53033	0.46884	0.41497	0.36770	0.32618	0.28967
14	0.86998	0.75788	0.66113	0.57748	0.50507	0.44231	0.38782	0.34046	0.29925	0.26333
15	0.86137	0.74302	0.64187	0.55527	0.48102	0.41727	0.36245	0.31524	0.27454	0.23940
16	0.85284	0.72846	0.62318	0.53391	0.45812	0.39365	0.33874	0.29189	0.25187	0.21763
17	0.84440	0.71417	0.60502	0.51338	0.43630	0.37137	0.31658	0.27027	0.23108	0.19785
18	0.83604	0.70017	0.58740	0.49363	0.41553	0.35035	0.29587	0.25025	0.21200	0.17986
19	0.82776	0.68644	0.57030	0.47465	0.39574	0.33052	0.27651	0.23171	0.19449	0.16351
20	0.81957	0.67298	0.55369	0.45639	0.37690	0.31181	0.25842	0.21455	0.17843	0.14865
21	0.81145	0.65979	0.53756	0.43884	0.35895	0.29416	0.24152	0.19866	0.16370	0.13513
22	0.80342	0.64685	0.52190	0.42196	0.34186	0.27751	0.22572	0.18394	0.15018	0.12285
23	0.79547	0.63417	0.50670	0.40573	0.32558	0.26180	0.21095	0.17032	0.13779	0.11168
24	0.78759	0.62173	0.49194	0.39013	0.31008	0.24698	0.19715	0.15770	0.12641	0.10153
25	0.77979	0.60954	0.47762	0.37512	0.29531	0.23300	0.18425	0.14602	0.11597	0.09230
26	0.77207	0.59759	0.46370	0.36069	0.28125	0.21982	0.17220	0.13520	0.10640	0.08391
27	0.76443	0.58588	0.45020	0.34682	0.26786	0.20737	0.16093	0.12519	0.09761	0.07628
28	0.75686	0.57439	0.43709	0.33348	0.25510	0.19564	0.15041	0.11592	0.08955	0.06935
29	0.74937	0.56313	0.42436	0.32066	0.24295	0.18456	0.14057	0.10733	0.08216	0.06304
30	0.74195	0.55208	0.41200	0.30832	0.23138	0.17412	0.13137	0.09938	0.07537	0.05731

TABLE B1 -- PRESENT VALUE OF $1 DUE AT THE END OF N YEARS

INTEREST RATES

N	0.11	0.12	0.13	0.14	0.15	0.16	0.17	0.18	0.19	0.20
1	0.90090	0.89286	0.88496	0.87719	0.86957	0.86207	0.85470	0.84746	0.84034	0.83333
2	0.81162	0.79719	0.78315	0.76947	0.75614	0.74316	0.73051	0.71819	0.70617	0.69445
3	0.73119	0.71178	0.69305	0.67497	0.65752	0.64066	0.62437	0.60863	0.59342	0.57870
4	0.65873	0.63552	0.61332	0.59208	0.57175	0.55229	0.53365	0.51579	0.49867	0.48225
5	0.59345	0.56743	0.54276	0.51937	0.49718	0.47611	0.45611	0.43711	0.41905	0.40188
6	0.53464	0.50663	0.48032	0.45559	0.43233	0.41044	0.38984	0.37043	0.35214	0.33490
7	0.48166	0.45235	0.42506	0.39964	0.37594	0.35383	0.33320	0.31393	0.29592	0.27908
8	0.43393	0.40388	0.37616	0.35056	0.32690	0.30503	0.28478	0.26604	0.24867	0.23257
9	0.39093	0.36061	0.33289	0.30751	0.28426	0.26295	0.24341	0.22546	0.20897	0.19381
10	0.35219	0.32197	0.29459	0.26975	0.24719	0.22668	0.20804	0.19107	0.17560	0.16151
11	0.31729	0.28748	0.26070	0.23662	0.21494	0.19542	0.17781	0.16192	0.14757	0.13459
12	0.28584	0.25668	0.23071	0.20756	0.18691	0.16846	0.15198	0.13722	0.12401	0.11216
13	0.25752	0.22918	0.20417	0.18207	0.16253	0.14523	0.12989	0.11629	0.10421	0.09346
14	0.23200	0.20462	0.18068	0.15971	0.14133	0.12520	0.11102	0.09855	0.08757	0.07789
15	0.20901	0.18270	0.15989	0.14010	0.12290	0.10793	0.09489	0.08352	0.07359	0.06491
16	0.18829	0.16312	0.14150	0.12289	0.10687	0.09304	0.08110	0.07078	0.06184	0.05409
17	0.16963	0.14565	0.12522	0.10780	0.09293	0.08021	0.06932	0.05998	0.05196	0.04507
18	0.15282	0.13004	0.11081	0.09456	0.08081	0.06914	0.05925	0.05083	0.04367	0.03756
19	0.13768	0.11611	0.09807	0.08295	0.07027	0.05961	0.05064	0.04308	0.03670	0.03130
20	0.12404	0.10367	0.08678	0.07276	0.06110	0.05139	0.04329	0.03651	0.03084	0.02608
21	0.11174	0.09256	0.07680	0.06383	0.05313	0.04430	0.03699	0.03094	0.02591	0.02174
22	0.10067	0.08264	0.06796	0.05599	0.04620	0.03819	0.03162	0.02622	0.02178	0.01811
23	0.09069	0.07379	0.06015	0.04911	0.04018	0.03292	0.02702	0.02222	0.01830	0.01510
24	0.08171	0.06588	0.05323	0.04308	0.03493	0.02838	0.02310	0.01883	0.01538	0.01258
25	0.07361	0.05882	0.04710	0.03779	0.03038	0.02447	0.01974	0.01596	0.01292	0.01048
26	0.06631	0.05252	0.04168	0.03315	0.02642	0.02109	0.01687	0.01352	0.01086	0.00874
27	0.05974	0.04689	0.03689	0.02908	0.02297	0.01818	0.01442	0.01146	0.00913	0.00728
28	0.05382	0.04187	0.03265	0.02551	0.01997	0.01567	0.01233	0.00971	0.00767	0.00607
29	0.04849	0.03738	0.02889	0.02238	0.01737	0.01351	0.01053	0.00823	0.00644	0.00506
30	0.04368	0.03338	0.02557	0.01963	0.01510	0.01165	0.00900	0.00698	0.00542	0.00421

TABLE B1 -- PRESENT VALUE OF $1 DUE AT THE END OF N YEARS

INTEREST RATES

N	0.21	0.22	0.23	0.24	0.25	0.26	0.27	0.28	0.29	0.30
1	0.82645	0.81967	0.81301	0.80645	0.80000	0.79365	0.78740	0.78125	0.77519	0.76923
2	0.68301	0.67186	0.66098	0.65036	0.64000	0.62988	0.62000	0.61035	0.60093	0.59172
3	0.56448	0.55071	0.53738	0.52449	0.51200	0.49991	0.48819	0.47684	0.46583	0.45517
4	0.46651	0.45140	0.43690	0.42297	0.40960	0.39675	0.38440	0.37253	0.36111	0.35013
5	0.38555	0.37000	0.35520	0.34111	0.32768	0.31488	0.30268	0.29104	0.27993	0.26933
6	0.31863	0.30328	0.28878	0.27509	0.26214	0.24991	0.23833	0.22737	0.21700	0.20718
7	0.26333	0.24859	0.23478	0.22185	0.20972	0.19834	0.18766	0.17764	0.16822	0.15937
8	0.21763	0.20376	0.19088	0.17891	0.16777	0.15741	0.14777	0.13878	0.13040	0.12259
9	0.17986	0.16702	0.15519	0.14428	0.13422	0.12493	0.11635	0.10842	0.10109	0.09430
10	0.14865	0.13690	0.12617	0.11636	0.10737	0.09915	0.09161	0.08470	0.07836	0.07254
11	0.12285	0.11221	0.10258	0.09383	0.08590	0.07869	0.07214	0.06617	0.06075	0.05580
12	0.10153	0.09198	0.08340	0.07567	0.06872	0.06245	0.05680	0.05170	0.04709	0.04292
13	0.08391	0.07539	0.06780	0.06103	0.05498	0.04957	0.04473	0.04039	0.03650	0.03302
14	0.06934	0.06180	0.05512	0.04922	0.04396	0.03934	0.03522	0.03155	0.02830	0.02540
15	0.05731	0.05065	0.04482	0.03969	0.03518	0.03122	0.02773	0.02465	0.02194	0.01954
16	0.04736	0.04152	0.03644	0.03201	0.02815	0.02478	0.02183	0.01926	0.01700	0.01503
17	0.03914	0.03403	0.02962	0.02581	0.02252	0.01967	0.01719	0.01505	0.01318	0.01156
18	0.03235	0.02790	0.02408	0.02082	0.01801	0.01561	0.01354	0.01176	0.01022	0.00889
19	0.02674	0.02286	0.01958	0.01679	0.01441	0.01239	0.01066	0.00918	0.00792	0.00684
20	0.02210	0.01874	0.01592	0.01354	0.01153	0.00983	0.00839	0.00717	0.00614	0.00526
21	0.01826	0.01536	0.01294	0.01092	0.00922	0.00780	0.00661	0.00561	0.00476	0.00405
22	0.01509	0.01259	0.01052	0.00880	0.00738	0.00619	0.00520	0.00438	0.00369	0.00311
23	0.01247	0.01032	0.00855	0.00710	0.00590	0.00491	0.00410	0.00342	0.00286	0.00240
24	0.01031	0.00846	0.00695	0.00573	0.00472	0.00390	0.00323	0.00267	0.00222	0.00184
25	0.00852	0.00693	0.00565	0.00462	0.00378	0.00310	0.00254	0.00209	0.00172	0.00142
26	0.00704	0.00568	0.00460	0.00372	0.00302	0.00246	0.00200	0.00163	0.00133	0.00109
27	0.00582	0.00466	0.00374	0.00300	0.00242	0.00155	0.00158	0.00127	0.00103	0.00084
28	0.00481	0.00382	0.00304	0.00242	0.00193	0.00155	0.00124	0.00100	0.00080	0.00065
29	0.00397	0.00313	0.00247	0.00195	0.00155	0.00123	0.00098	0.00078	0.00062	0.00050
30	0.00328	0.00257	0.00201	0.00158	0.00124	0.00097	0.00077	0.00061	0.00048	0.00038

TABLE B1 -- PRESENT VALUE OF $1 DUE AT THE END OF N YEARS

INTEREST RATES

N	0.31	0.32	0.33	0.34	0.35	0.36	0.37	0.38	0.39	0.40
1	0.76336	0.75758	0.75188	0.74627	0.74074	0.73529	0.72993	0.72464	0.71942	0.71429
2	0.58272	0.57392	0.56532	0.55692	0.54870	0.54066	0.53279	0.52510	0.51757	0.51020
3	0.44482	0.43479	0.42506	0.41561	0.40644	0.39754	0.38890	0.38051	0.37235	0.36443
4	0.33956	0.32939	0.31959	0.31016	0.30107	0.29231	0.28387	0.27573	0.26788	0.26031
5	0.25921	0.24953	0.24029	0.23146	0.22301	0.21493	0.20723	0.19980	0.19272	0.18593
6	0.19787	0.18904	0.18067	0.17273	0.16520	0.15804	0.15124	0.14479	0.13865	0.13281
7	0.15104	0.14321	0.13584	0.12890	0.12237	0.11621	0.11040	0.10492	0.09975	0.09486
8	0.11530	0.10850	0.10214	0.09620	0.09064	0.08545	0.08058	0.07603	0.07176	0.06776
9	0.08802	0.08219	0.07680	0.07179	0.06714	0.06283	0.05882	0.05509	0.05163	0.04840
10	0.06719	0.06227	0.05774	0.05357	0.04974	0.04620	0.04293	0.03992	0.03714	0.03457
11	0.05129	0.04717	0.04341	0.03998	0.03684	0.03397	0.03134	0.02893	0.02672	0.02469
12	0.03915	0.03574	0.03264	0.02984	0.02729	0.02498	0.02287	0.02096	0.01922	0.01764
13	0.02989	0.02707	0.02454	0.02227	0.02021	0.01837	0.01670	0.01519	0.01383	0.01260
14	0.02281	0.02051	0.01845	0.01662	0.01497	0.01350	0.01219	0.01101	0.00995	0.00900
15	0.01742	0.01554	0.01387	0.01240	0.01109	0.00993	0.00890	0.00798	0.00716	0.00643
16	0.01329	0.01177	0.01043	0.00925	0.00822	0.00730	0.00649	0.00578	0.00515	0.00459
17	0.01015	0.00892	0.00784	0.00691	0.00609	0.00537	0.00474	0.00419	0.00370	0.00328
18	0.00775	0.00676	0.00590	0.00515	0.00451	0.00395	0.00346	0.00304	0.00267	0.00234
19	0.00591	0.00512	0.00443	0.00385	0.00334	0.00290	0.00253	0.00220	0.00192	0.00167
20	0.00451	0.00388	0.00333	0.00287	0.00247	0.00213	0.00184	0.00159	0.00138	0.00120
21	0.00345	0.00294	0.00251	0.00214	0.00183	0.00157	0.00135	0.00115	0.00099	0.00085
22	0.00263	0.00223	0.00188	0.00160	0.00136	0.00115	0.00098	0.00084	0.00071	0.00061
23	0.00201	0.00169	0.00142	0.00119	0.00101	0.00085	0.00072	0.00061	0.00051	0.00044
24	0.00153	0.00128	0.00107	0.00089	0.00074	0.00062	0.00052	0.00044	0.00037	0.00031
25	0.00117	0.00097	0.00080	0.00066	0.00055	0.00046	0.00038	0.00032	0.00027	0.00022
26	0.00089	0.00073	0.00060	0.00050	0.00041	0.00034	0.00028	0.00023	0.00019	0.00016
27	0.00068	0.00056	0.00045	0.00037	0.00030	0.00025	0.00020	0.00017	0.00014	0.00011
28	0.00052	0.00042	0.00034	0.00028	0.00022	0.00018	0.00015	0.00012	0.00010	0.00008
29	0.00040	0.00032	0.00026	0.00021	0.00017	0.00013	0.00011	0.00009	0.00007	0.00006
30	0.00030	0.00024	0.00019	0.00015	0.00012	0.00010	0.00008	0.00006	0.00005	0.00004

TABLE B2 -- PRESENT VALUE OF $1 PER YEAR FOR N YEARS

INTEREST RATES

N	0.01	0.02	0.03	0.04	0.05	0.06	0.07	0.08	0.09	0.10
1	0.99010	0.98039	0.97087	0.96154	0.95238	0.94340	0.93458	0.92593	0.91743	0.90909
2	1.97040	1.94156	1.91347	1.88610	1.85941	1.83339	1.80802	1.78327	1.75911	1.73554
3	2.94099	2.88388	2.82861	2.77509	2.72325	2.67301	2.62432	2.57710	2.53130	2.48685
4	3.90197	3.80773	3.71710	3.62990	3.54595	3.46511	3.38722	3.31213	3.23972	3.16987
5	4.85345	4.71347	4.57971	4.45183	4.32949	4.21237	4.10020	3.99271	3.88966	3.79079
6	5.79550	5.60144	5.41720	5.24214	5.07571	4.91734	4.76655	4.62288	4.48593	4.35527
7	6.72822	6.47201	6.23030	6.00206	5.78639	5.58240	5.38930	5.20638	5.03297	4.86843
8	7.65172	7.32550	7.01971	6.73276	6.46324	6.20981	5.97131	5.74665	5.53484	5.33494
9	8.56607	8.16226	7.78613	7.43535	7.10785	6.80172	6.51525	6.24690	5.99527	5.75904
10	9.47136	8.98262	8.53023	8.11091	7.72177	7.36012	7.02360	6.71009	6.41768	6.14459
11	10.36770	9.78689	9.25266	8.76050	8.30646	7.88691	7.49870	7.13898	6.80522	6.49508
12	11.25516	10.57539	9.95405	9.38510	8.86330	8.38388	7.94271	7.53609	7.16076	6.81372
13	12.13384	11.34843	10.63500	9.98568	9.39363	8.85273	8.35768	7.90380	7.48694	7.10338
14	13.00382	12.10631	11.29613	10.56316	9.89870	9.29503	8.74550	8.24426	7.78619	7.36672
15	13.86518	12.84934	11.93800	11.11843	10.37973	9.71231	9.10795	8.55950	8.06073	7.60611
16	14.71802	13.57779	12.56117	11.65234	10.83784	10.10596	9.44669	8.85140	8.31261	7.82375
17	15.56242	14.29196	13.16620	12.16572	11.27415	10.47733	9.76327	9.12167	8.54368	8.02145
18	16.39845	14.99213	13.75360	12.65935	11.68968	10.82768	10.05914	9.37192	8.75568	8.20145
19	17.22621	15.67858	14.32389	13.13400	12.08542	11.15820	10.33565	9.63363	8.95017	8.36496
20	18.04578	16.35155	14.87758	13.59039	12.46231	11.47001	10.59407	9.81818	9.12861	8.51361
21	18.85722	17.01132	15.41514	14.02923	12.82126	11.76417	10.83559	10.01684	9.29231	8.64874
22	19.66063	17.65817	15.93704	14.45119	13.16312	12.04168	11.06131	10.20378	9.44249	8.77159
23	20.45609	18.29233	16.44375	14.85692	13.48870	12.30348	11.27226	10.37110	9.58028	8.88327
24	21.24367	18.91405	16.93567	15.24705	13.79877	12.55046	11.46941	10.52880	9.70668	8.98480
25	22.02345	19.52359	17.41328	15.62217	14.09408	12.78347	11.65366	10.67482	9.82265	9.07710
26	22.79552	20.12117	17.87698	15.98286	14.37531	13.00328	11.82586	10.81002	9.92905	9.16100
27	23.55994	20.70703	18.32718	16.32968	14.64319	13.21066	11.98679	10.93521	10.02666	9.23728
28	24.31679	21.28142	18.76425	16.66316	14.89829	13.40629	12.13720	11.05113	10.11621	9.30663
29	25.06615	21.84454	19.18860	16.98381	15.14124	13.59085	12.27776	11.15846	10.19837	9.36967
30	25.80809	22.39662	19.60059	17.29213	15.37262	13.76497	12.40913	11.25783	10.27374	9.42698

TABLE B2 -- PRESENT VALUE OF $1 PER YEAR FOR N YEARS

INTEREST RATES

N	0.11	0.12	0.13	0.14	0.15	0.16	0.17	0.18	0.19	0.20
1	0.90090	0.89286	0.88496	0.87719	0.86957	0.86207	0.85470	0.84746	0.84034	0.83333
2	1.71252	1.69005	1.66810	1.64666	1.62571	1.60523	1.58522	1.56564	1.54650	1.52778
3	2.44372	2.40183	2.36116	2.32163	2.28323	2.24589	2.20959	2.17428	2.13992	2.10648
4	3.10245	3.03735	2.97448	2.91372	2.85498	2.79818	2.74324	2.69007	2.63859	2.58873
5	3.69590	3.60478	3.51724	3.43309	3.35216	3.27430	3.19935	3.12718	3.05764	2.99061
6	4.23054	4.11141	3.99756	3.88868	3.78449	3.68474	3.58919	3.49761	3.40978	3.32551
7	4.71220	4.56376	4.42262	4.28832	4.16043	4.03857	3.92239	3.81154	3.70570	3.60459
8	5.14613	4.96764	4.79879	4.63888	4.48732	4.34359	4.20717	4.07758	3.95437	3.83716
9	5.53706	5.32826	5.13167	4.94639	4.77159	4.60655	4.45058	4.30303	4.16334	4.03097
10	5.88925	5.65023	5.42627	5.21613	5.01878	4.83323	4.65862	4.49410	4.33894	4.19248
11	6.20653	5.93771	5.68697	5.45275	5.23372	5.02865	4.83643	4.65602	4.48651	4.32706
12	6.49237	6.19438	5.91767	5.66031	5.42063	5.19711	4.98841	4.79324	4.61051	4.43922
13	6.74989	6.42356	6.12184	5.84239	5.58316	5.34234	5.11830	4.90953	4.71472	4.53268
14	6.98189	6.62818	6.30252	6.00210	5.72449	5.46753	5.22932	5.00808	4.80228	4.61057
15	7.19089	6.81087	6.46241	6.14220	5.84739	5.57546	5.32421	5.09159	4.87587	4.67548
16	7.37919	6.97400	6.60391	6.26509	5.95425	5.66850	5.40531	5.16237	4.93771	4.72956
17	7.54882	7.11964	6.72913	6.37289	6.04718	5.74871	5.47463	5.22235	4.98967	4.77464
18	7.70164	7.24968	6.83995	6.46741	6.12799	5.81785	5.53387	5.27318	5.03334	4.81220
19	7.83932	7.36579	6.93801	6.55040	6.19825	5.87746	5.58451	5.31626	5.07003	4.84350
20	7.96336	7.46946	7.02479	6.62317	6.25935	5.92885	5.62779	5.35276	5.10087	4.86958
21	8.07510	7.56202	7.10159	6.68699	6.31248	5.97315	5.66478	5.38370	5.12678	4.89132
22	8.17577	7.64466	7.16956	6.74298	6.35868	6.01133	5.69640	5.40992	5.14856	4.90943
23	8.26646	7.71845	7.22970	6.79209	6.39886	6.04425	5.72342	5.43214	5.16685	4.92453
24	8.34817	7.78433	7.28293	6.83517	6.43379	6.07263	5.74652	5.45097	5.18223	4.93711
25	8.42178	7.84315	7.33003	6.87296	6.46417	6.09710	5.76626	5.46692	5.19515	4.94759
26	8.48809	7.89567	7.37172	6.90611	6.49058	6.11819	5.78313	5.48045	5.20601	4.95632
27	8.54784	7.94257	7.40861	6.93515	6.51355	6.13637	5.79755	5.49191	5.21514	4.96360
28	8.60166	7.98444	7.44125	6.96070	6.53353	6.15204	5.80987	5.50162	5.22280	4.96967
29	8.65015	8.02182	7.47014	6.98308	6.55090	6.16556	5.82041	5.50985	5.22925	4.97472
30	8.69383	8.05520	7.49570	7.00273	6.56600	6.17720	5.82941	5.51682	5.23466	4.97894

TABLE B2 -- PRESENT VALUE OF $1 PER YEAR FOR N YEARS

INTEREST RATES

N	0.21	0.22	0.23	0.24	0.25	0.26	0.27	0.28	0.29	0.30
1	0.82645	0.81967	0.81301	0.80645	0.80000	0.79365	0.78740	0.78125	0.77519	0.76923
2	1.50946	1.49154	1.47399	1.45682	1.44000	1.42353	1.40740	1.39160	1.37612	1.36095
3	2.07394	2.04224	2.01137	1.98130	1.95200	1.92344	1.89559	1.86844	1.84195	1.81611
4	2.54045	2.49364	2.44827	2.40428	2.36160	2.32019	2.28000	2.24097	2.20306	2.16624
5	2.92599	2.86364	2.80347	2.74539	2.68928	2.63507	2.58267	2.53201	2.48299	2.43557
6	3.24462	3.16692	3.09226	3.02047	2.95142	2.88498	2.82100	2.75938	2.70000	2.64275
7	3.50795	3.41551	3.32704	3.24232	3.16114	3.08332	3.00867	2.93702	2.86821	2.80212
8	3.72558	3.61927	3.51792	3.42122	3.32891	3.24073	3.15643	3.07579	2.99861	2.92471
9	3.90545	3.78629	3.67311	3.56550	3.46312	3.36566	3.27278	3.18421	3.09970	3.01900
10	4.05409	3.92319	3.79927	3.68186	3.57050	3.46481	3.36440	3.26892	3.17806	3.09154
11	4.17694	4.03540	3.90185	3.77569	3.65640	3.54350	3.43653	3.33509	3.23881	3.14734
12	4.27846	4.12738	3.98524	3.85137	3.72511	3.60595	3.49333	3.38679	3.28589	3.19026
13	4.36237	4.20277	4.05304	3.91239	3.78009	3.65552	3.53806	3.42718	3.32240	3.22328
14	4.43171	4.26457	4.10817	3.96161	3.82407	3.69486	3.57328	3.45873	3.35069	3.24868
15	4.48902	4.31522	4.15298	4.00130	3.85925	3.72608	3.60100	3.48339	3.37263	3.26821
16	4.53638	4.35674	4.18942	4.03330	3.88740	3.75086	3.62284	3.50264	3.38963	3.28324
17	4.57553	4.39077	4.21904	4.05911	3.90992	3.77052	3.64003	3.51769	3.40281	3.29480
18	4.60788	4.41867	4.24312	4.07993	3.92793	3.78613	3.65357	3.52944	3.41303	3.30369
19	4.63461	4.44153	4.26270	4.09672	3.94234	3.79852	3.66423	3.53863	3.42103	3.31053
20	4.65671	4.46027	4.27862	4.11026	3.95387	3.80835	3.67262	3.54580	3.42709	3.31579
21	4.67497	4.47564	4.29156	4.12117	3.96309	3.81615	3.67923	3.55141	3.43185	3.31984
22	4.69006	4.48823	4.30208	4.12998	3.97047	3.82234	3.68443	3.55579	3.43554	3.32296
23	4.70253	4.49855	4.31063	4.13708	3.97638	3.82725	3.68853	3.55921	3.43840	3.32535
24	4.71284	4.50701	4.31759	4.14280	3.98110	3.83115	3.69175	3.56188	3.44062	3.32719
25	4.72135	4.51394	4.32324	4.14742	3.98487	3.83425	3.69429	3.56397	3.44234	3.32861
26	4.72839	4.51963	4.32784	4.15115	3.98790	3.83671	3.69629	3.56560	3.44367	3.32970
27	4.73421	4.52428	4.33157	4.15415	3.99031	3.83865	3.69787	3.56687	3.44470	3.33054
28	4.73902	4.52810	4.33461	4.15657	3.99225	3.84020	3.69911	3.56787	3.44550	3.33118
29	4.74300	4.53123	4.33708	4.15852	3.99380	3.84143	3.70000	3.56864	3.44612	3.33168
30	4.74628	4.53380	4.33909	4.16010	3.99503	3.84240	3.70085	3.56925	3.44660	3.33206

INTEREST RATES

N	0.31	0.32	0.33	0.34	0.35	0.36	0.37	0.38	0.39	0.40
1	0.76336	0.75758	0.75188	0.74627	0.74074	0.73529	0.72993	0.72464	0.71942	0.71429
2	1.34608	1.33150	1.31720	1.30319	1.28944	1.27595	1.26272	1.24974	1.23700	1.22449
3	1.79090	1.76629	1.74226	1.71880	1.69588	1.67349	1.65162	1.63025	1.60935	1.58892
4	2.13046	2.09567	2.06185	2.02895	1.99695	1.96580	1.93549	1.90598	1.87723	1.84923
5	2.38966	2.34521	2.30214	2.26041	2.21996	2.18074	2.14269	2.10578	2.06995	2.03516
6	2.58753	2.53425	2.48281	2.43315	2.38516	2.33878	2.29393	2.25057	2.20860	2.16797
7	2.73857	2.67746	2.61866	2.56205	2.50753	2.45498	2.40433	2.35548	2.30834	2.26284
8	2.85387	2.78596	2.72079	2.65825	2.59817	2.54043	2.48491	2.43151	2.38013	2.33060
9	2.94189	2.86815	2.79759	2.73004	2.66531	2.60326	2.54373	2.48660	2.43173	2.37900
10	3.00908	2.93042	2.85533	2.78361	2.71504	2.64945	2.58666	2.52652	2.46887	2.41357
11	3.06036	2.97759	2.89874	2.82359	2.75189	2.68342	2.61800	2.55545	2.49559	2.43826
12	3.09951	3.01332	2.93139	2.85343	2.77917	2.70840	2.64088	2.57642	2.51481	2.45590
13	3.12940	3.04040	2.95593	2.87569	2.79939	2.72676	2.65757	2.59161	2.52864	2.46850
14	3.15222	3.06091	2.97438	2.89231	2.81436	2.74026	2.66976	2.60261	2.53859	2.47750
15	3.16963	3.07644	2.98825	2.90471	2.82545	2.75019	2.67865	2.61059	2.54575	2.48393
16	3.18292	3.08821	2.99869	2.91396	2.83367	2.75749	2.68515	2.61637	2.55090	2.48852
17	3.19307	3.09713	3.00653	2.92087	2.83976	2.76286	2.68989	2.62056	2.55460	2.49180
18	3.20082	3.10388	3.01243	2.92602	2.84426	2.76681	2.69335	2.62359	2.55727	2.49414
19	3.20673	3.10900	3.01696	2.92986	2.84760	2.76971	2.69587	2.62577	2.55918	2.49581
20	3.21125	3.11288	3.02019	2.93273	2.85007	2.77184	2.69771	2.62738	2.56056	2.49701
21	3.21469	3.11582	3.02270	2.93487	2.85191	2.77341	2.69906	2.62854	2.56155	2.49786
22	3.21732	3.11804	3.02458	2.93647	2.85326	2.77457	2.70004	2.62938	2.56227	2.49847
23	3.21933	3.11973	3.02600	2.93766	2.85427	2.77541	2.70075	2.62998	2.56278	2.49891
24	3.22086	3.12100	3.02707	2.93855	2.85501	2.77604	2.70128	2.63042	2.56315	2.49922
25	3.22203	3.12197	3.02787	2.93922	2.85556	2.77649	2.70166	2.63074	2.56341	2.49944
26	3.22292	3.12270	3.02847	2.93972	2.85598	2.77683	2.70194	2.63097	2.56360	2.49960
27	3.22360	3.12326	3.02892	2.94008	2.85627	2.77708	2.70214	2.63113	2.56374	2.49971
28	3.22412	3.12368	3.02926	2.94036	2.85650	2.77726	2.70229	2.63126	2.56384	2.49979
29	3.22452	3.12400	3.02952	2.94056	2.85666	2.77740	2.70240	2.63134	2.56391	2.49985
30	3.22482	3.12424	3.02971	2.94072	2.85679	2.77749	2.70247	2.63141	2.56396	2.49989